Come Into My Boudoir

a

Grayscale Erotic Adult Coloring Book

By

Ruby Chaste ♥

Hello beautiful! Hello handsome!

Welcome to my colorable boudoir collection. I hope you will enjoy coloring your way throughout as you take a journey back into the steamy past with this provocative collection of vintage boudoir grayscale coloring pages. The seductive allure that each of these temptresses possesses is unmistakable. Come hither as they beckon you into their enticing lair.

Grayscale coloring is addicting – you've been warned! Each of the antique/vintage images has been painstakingly refinished and retouched by artist and author, Ruby Chaste, making it ready for coloring. You add your own color and voila! The black and white shading that is already present on the print allows you to perfect your own color placement and create a gorgeous, frame worthy masterpiece! Important to note is the fact that because these prints are derived from antique and/or vintage photos, blurriness is innate to them.

Be sure and keep an eye out for future works of mine as more titles are in the works.

For now, though, whether your visit is solo, or with your special someone, gather all your favorite essentials, kick back, relax, and enjoy this creative and sensuous experience as you become your own 'InstantArteest'.

XOXO,

Ruby Chaste ♥

Art can never exist without naked beauty displayed.
~ William Blake

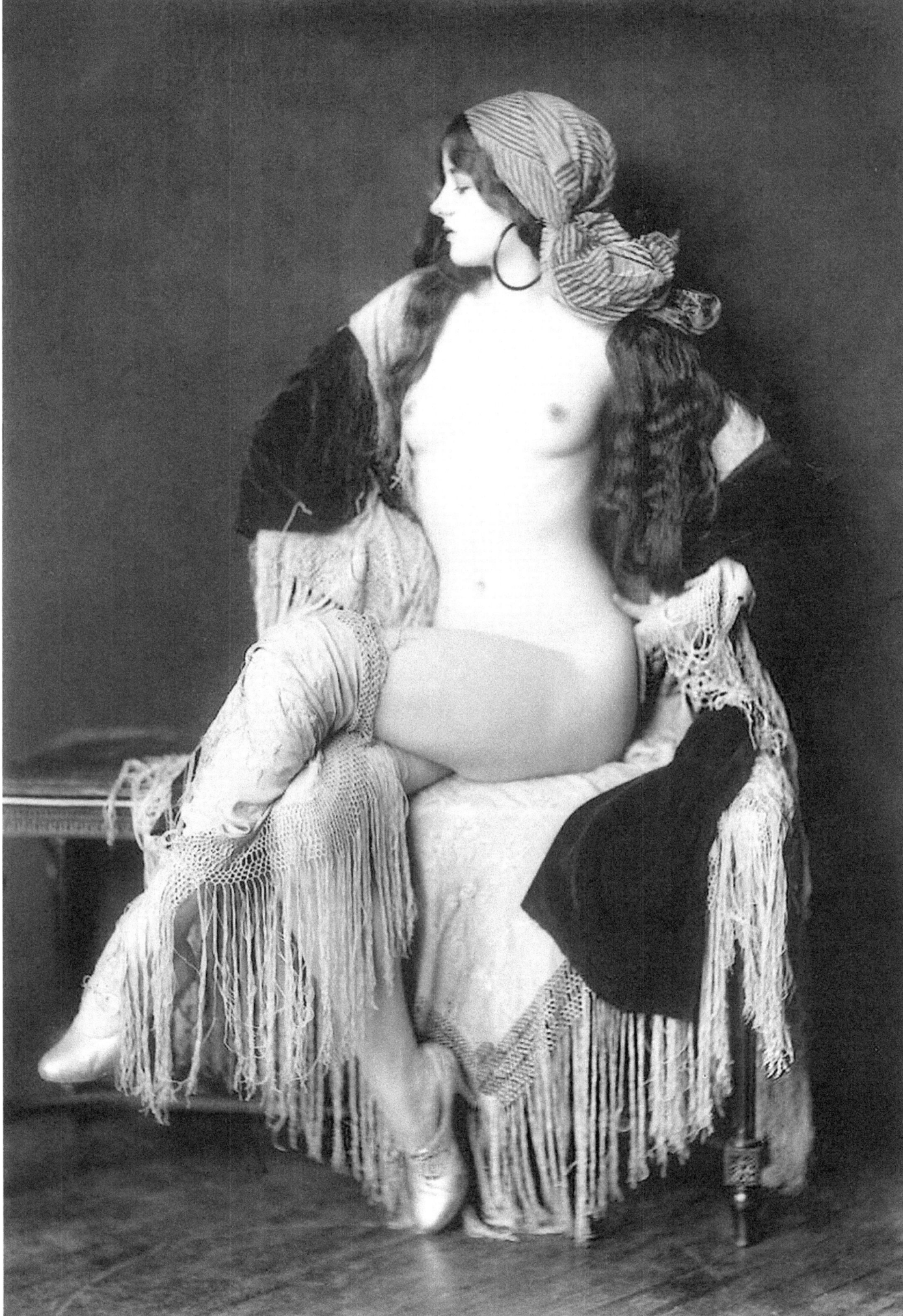

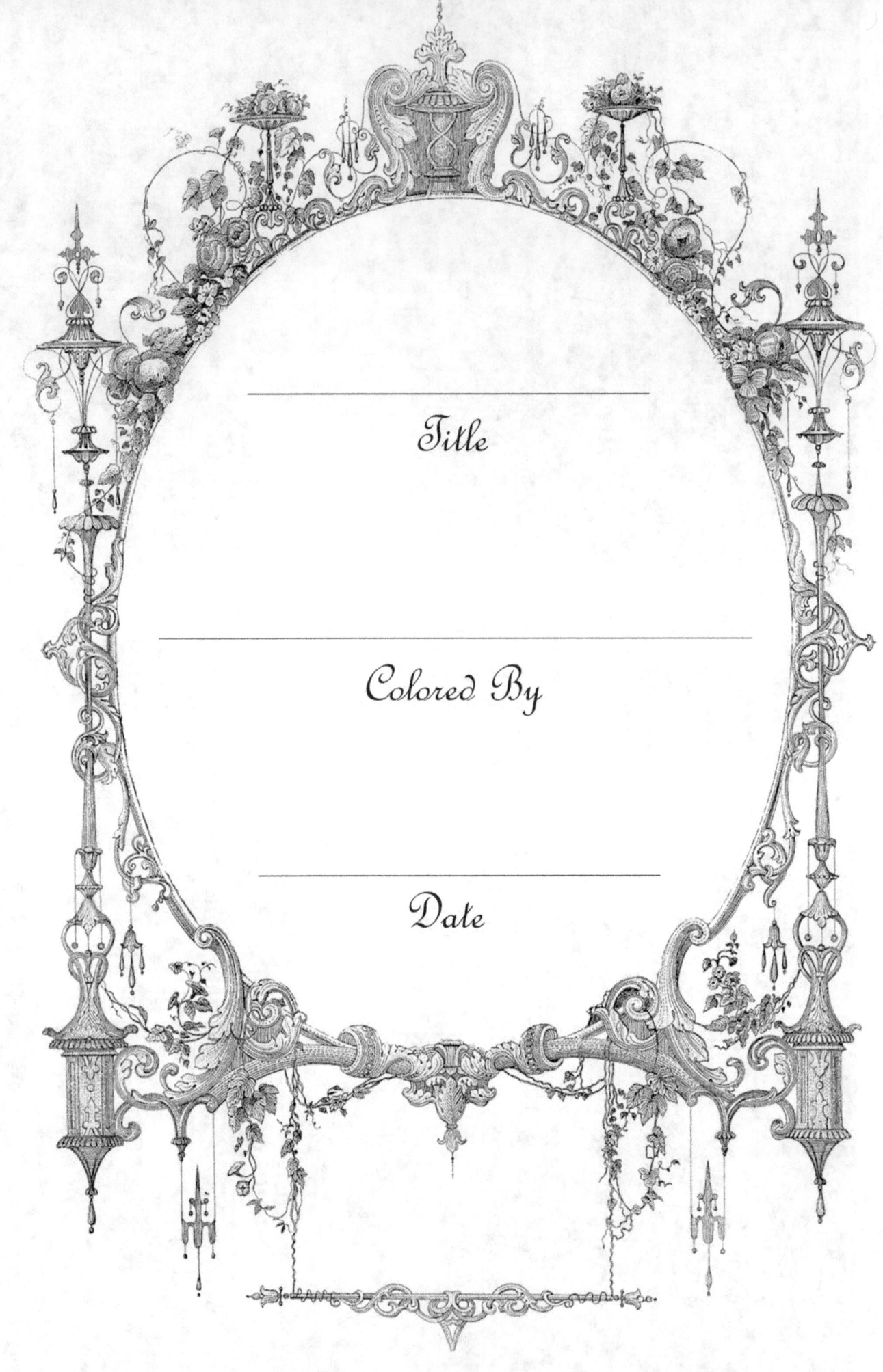

Title

Colored By

Date

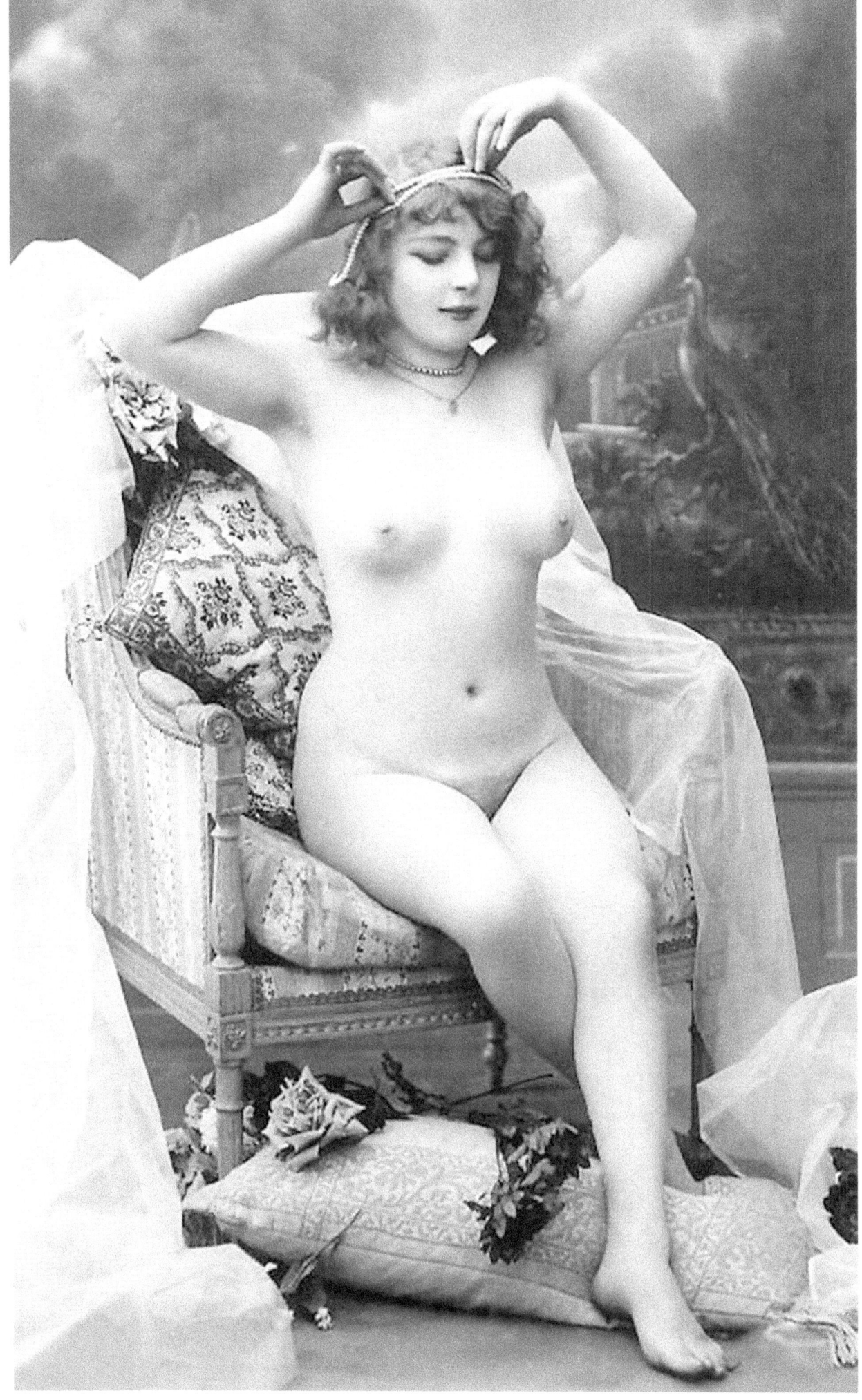

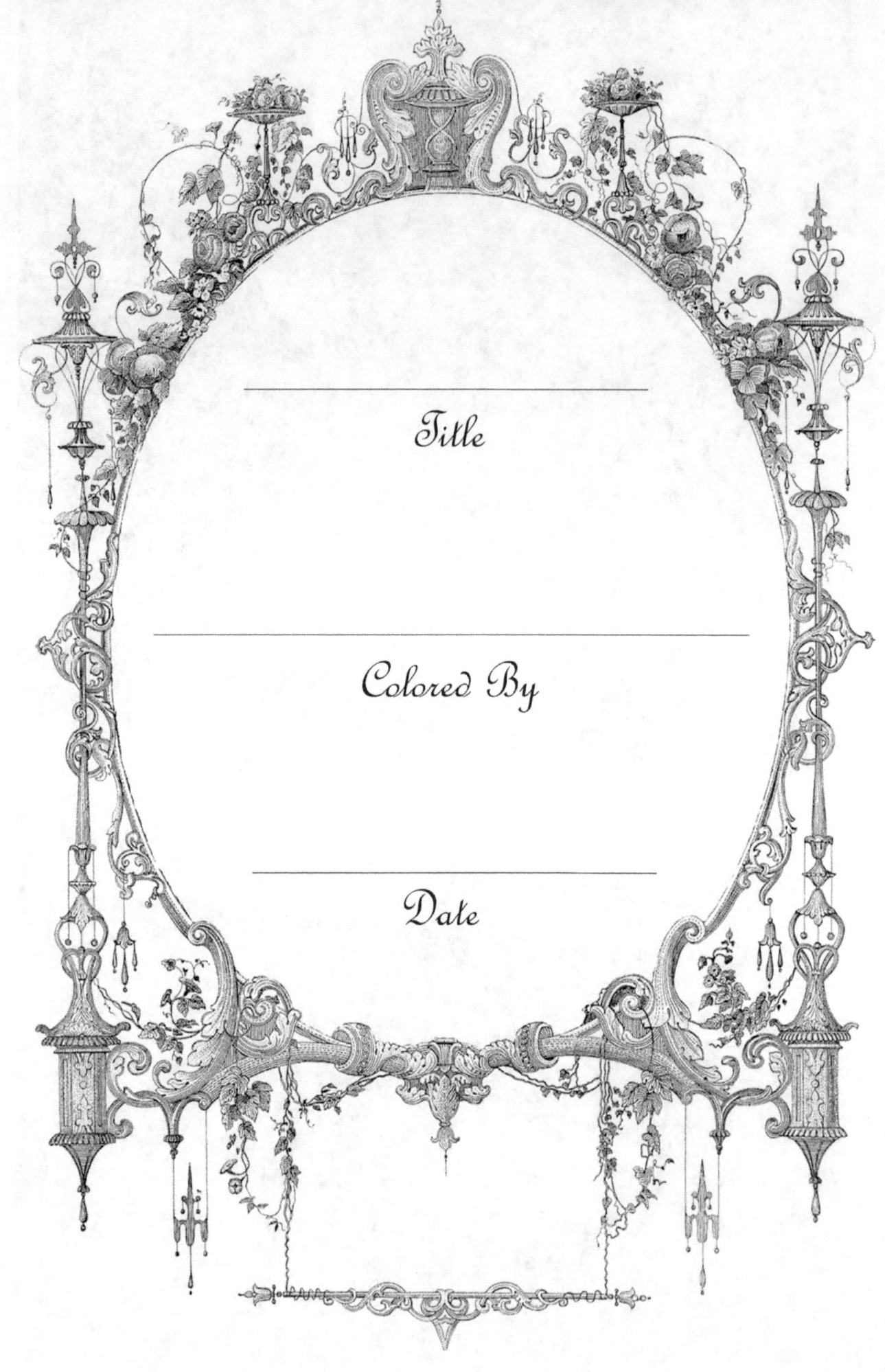

Title

Colored By

Date

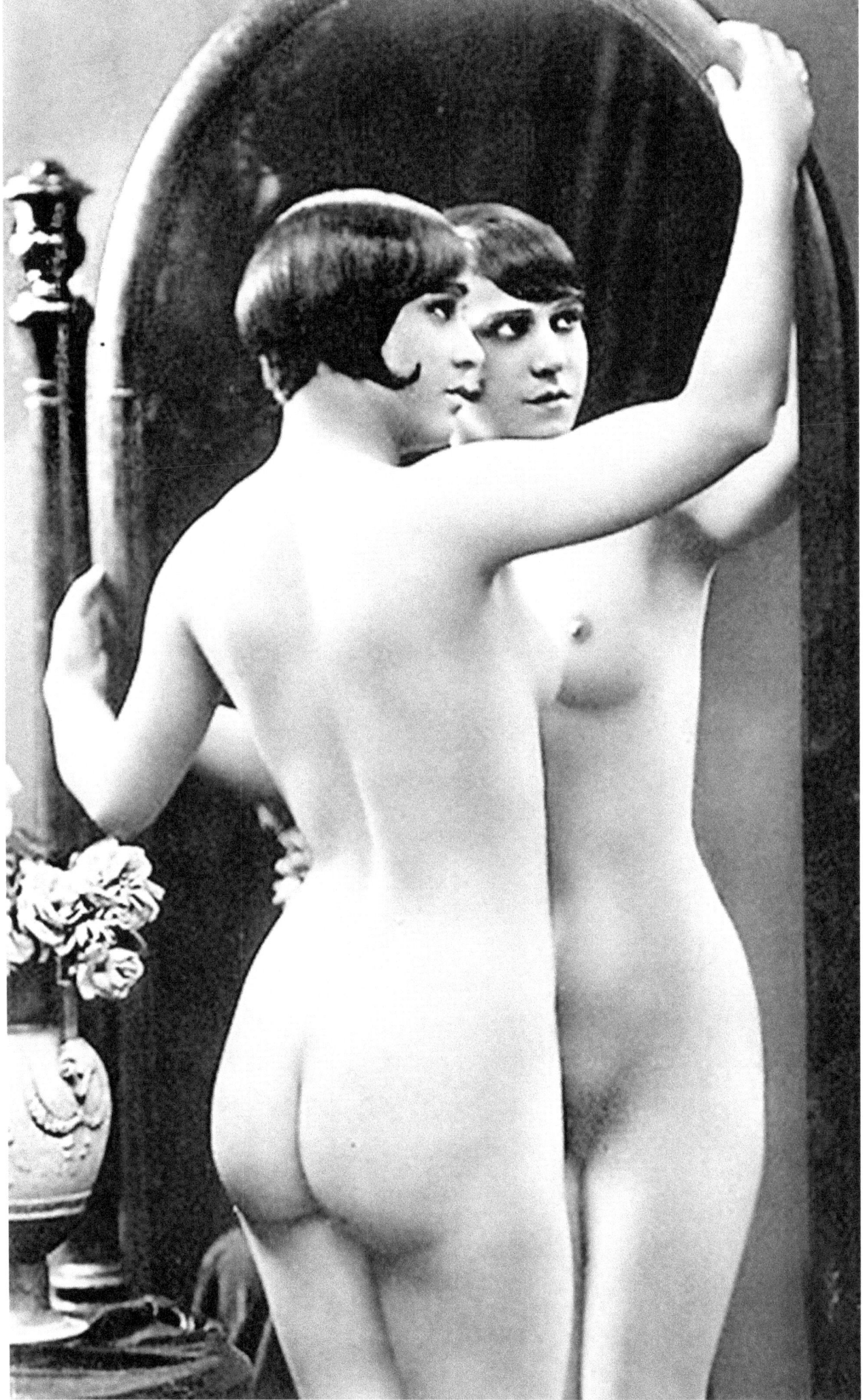

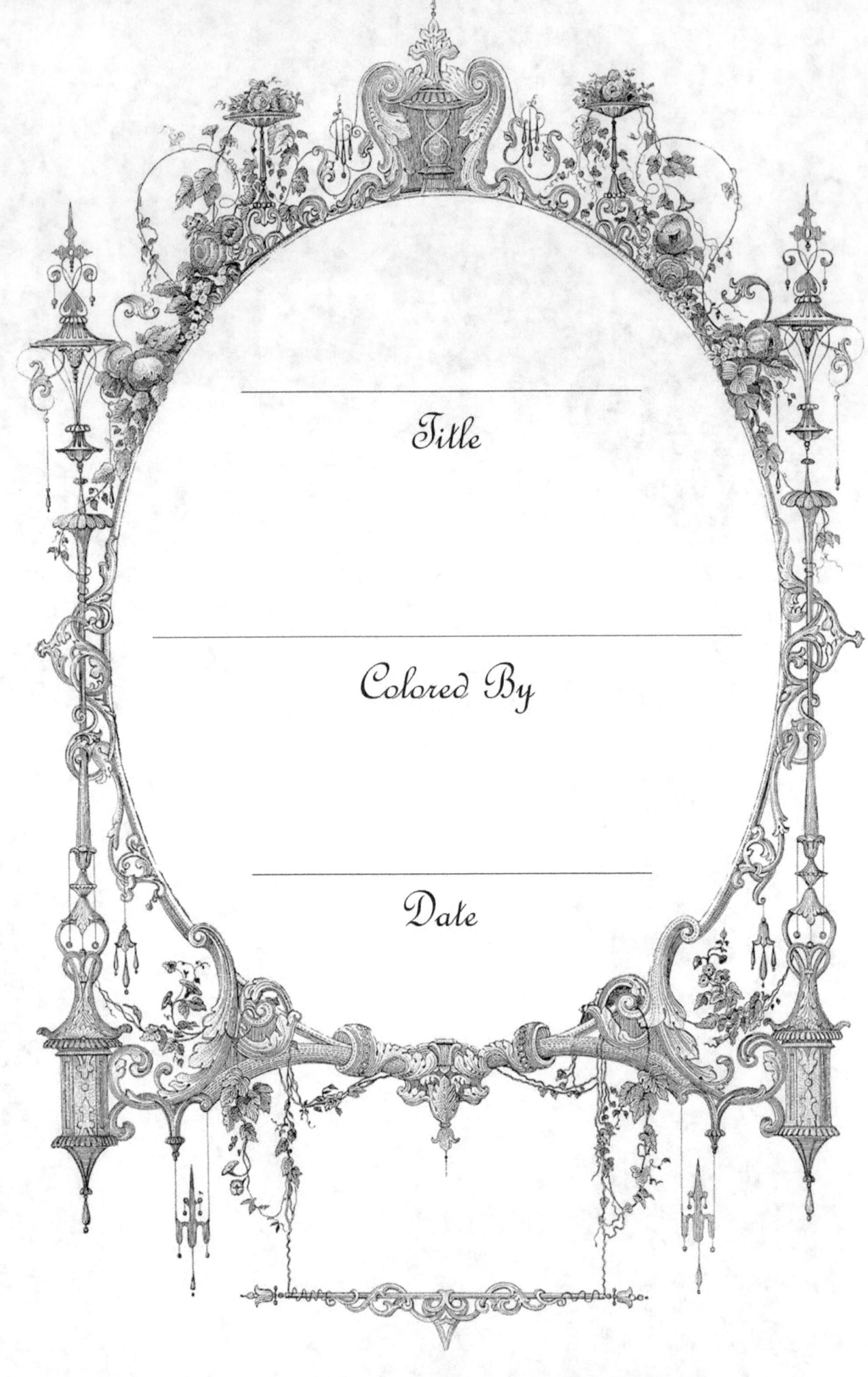

Title

Colored By

Date

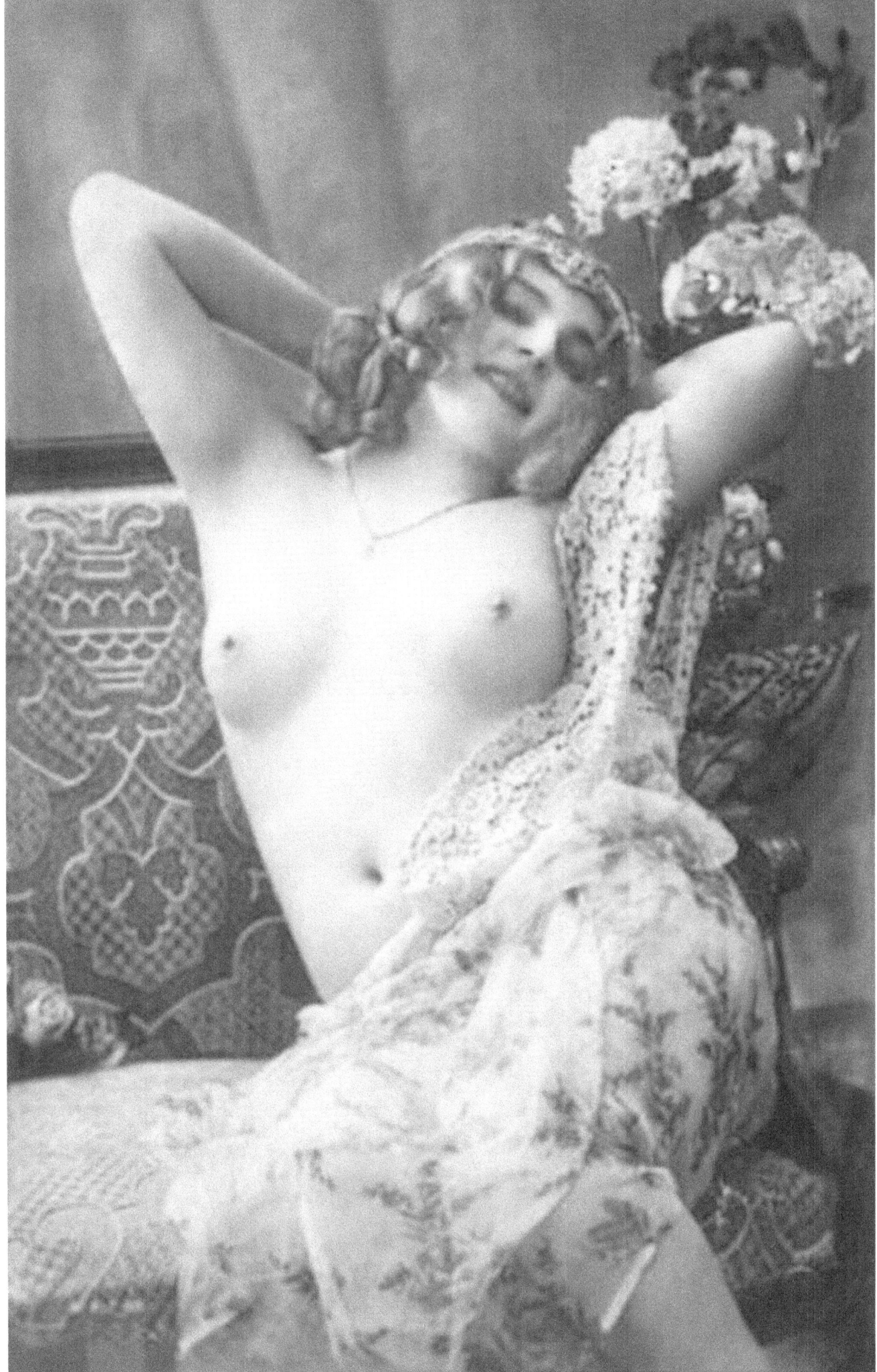

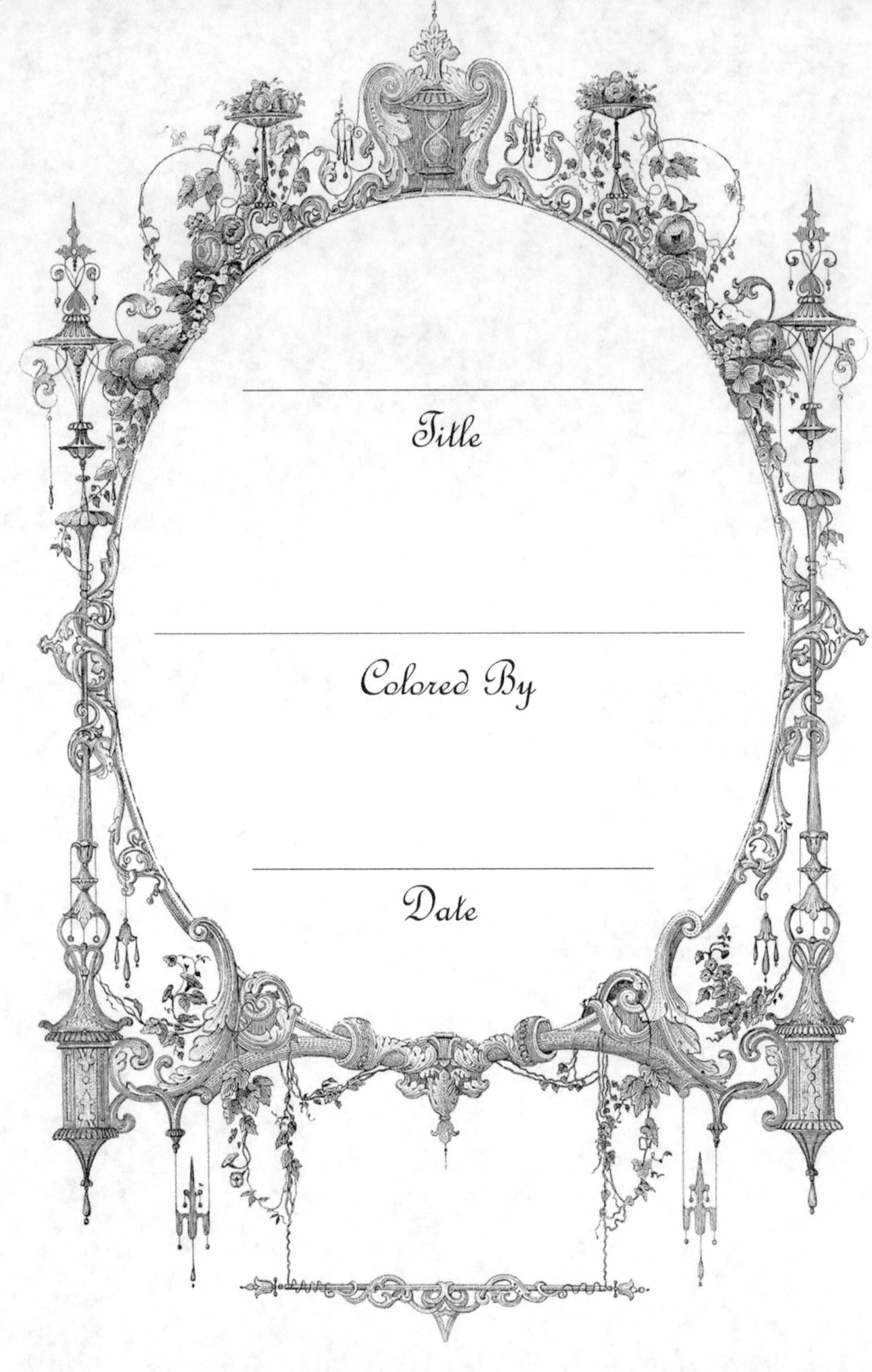

Title

Colored By

Date

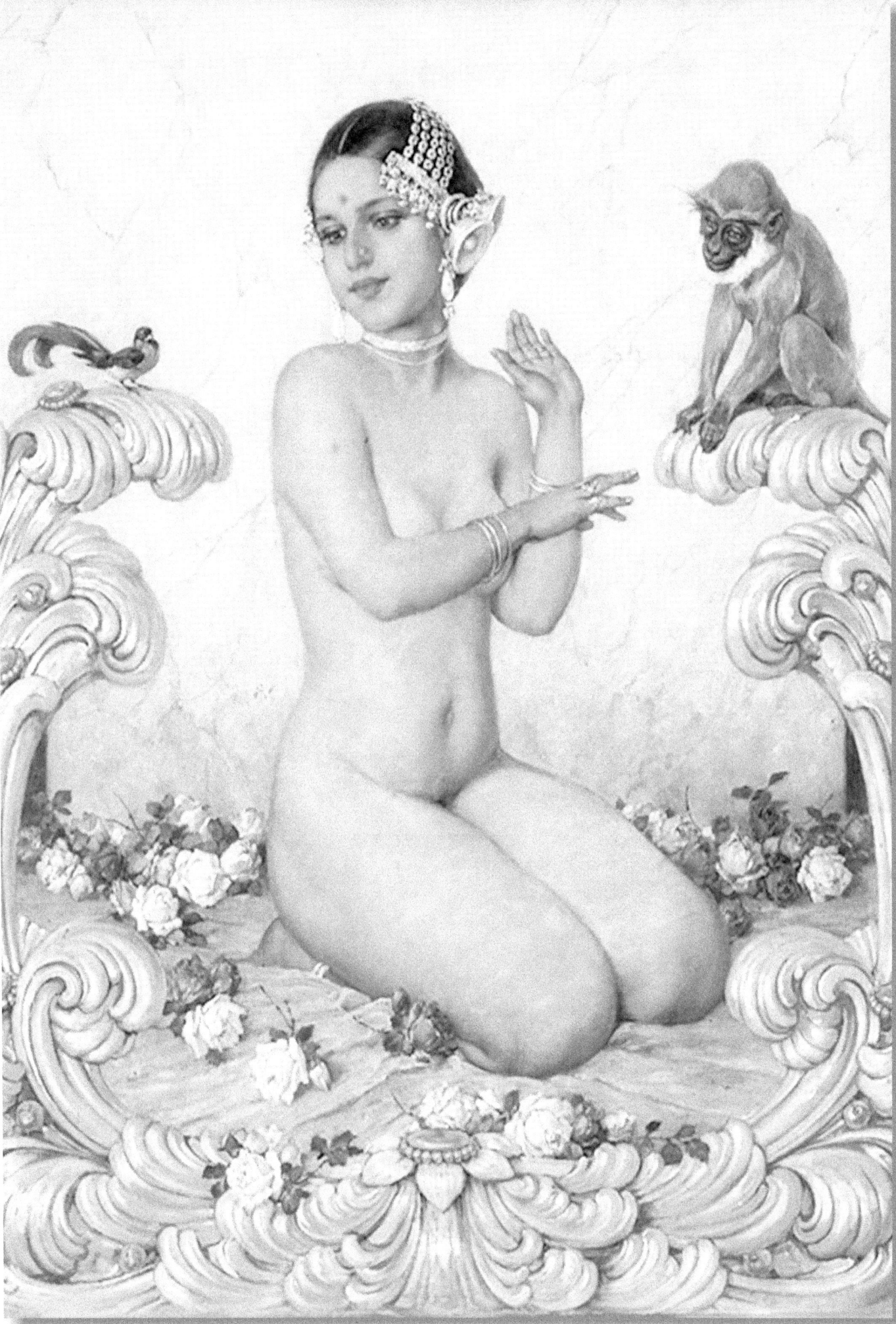

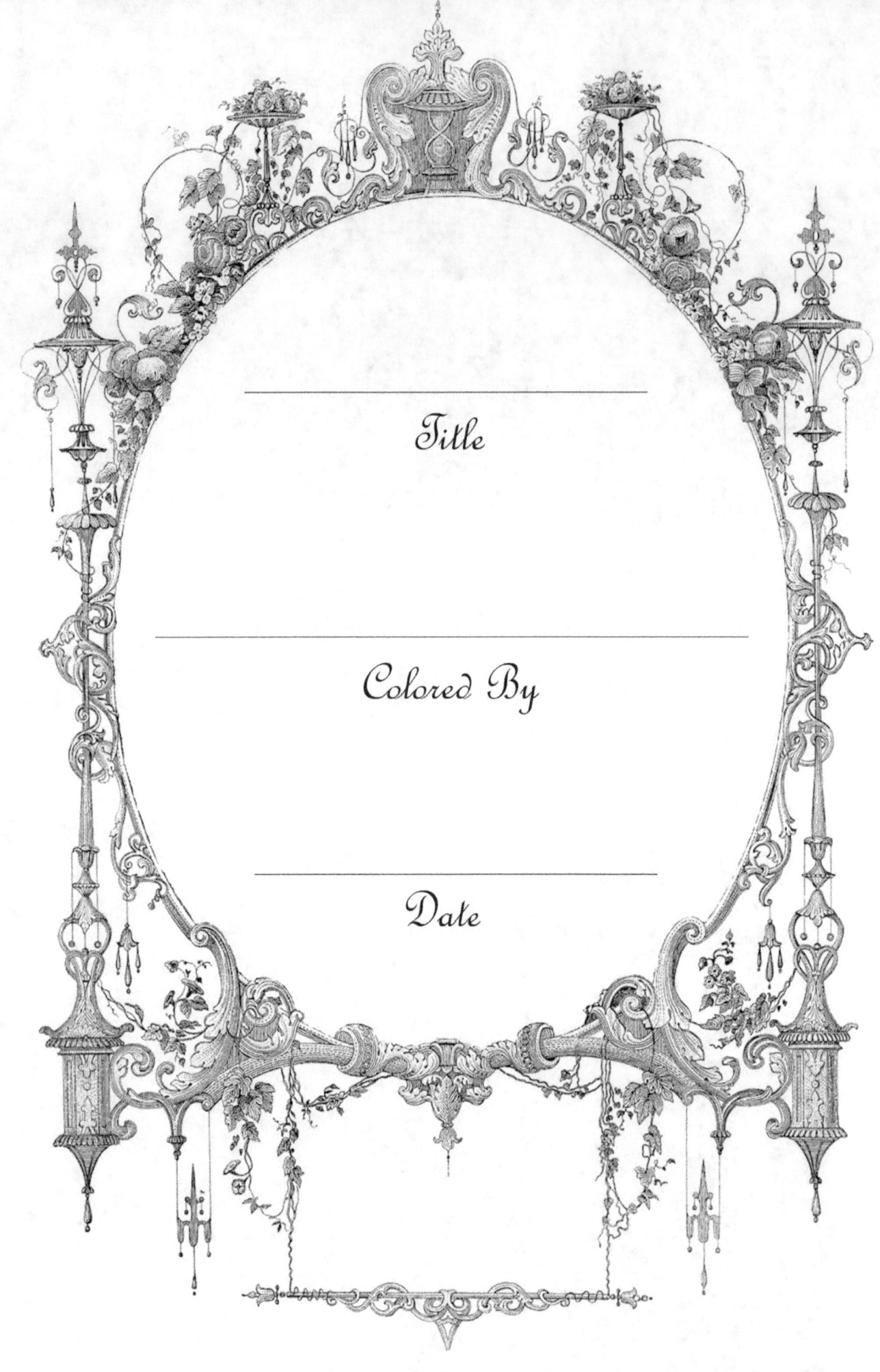

Title

Colored By

Date

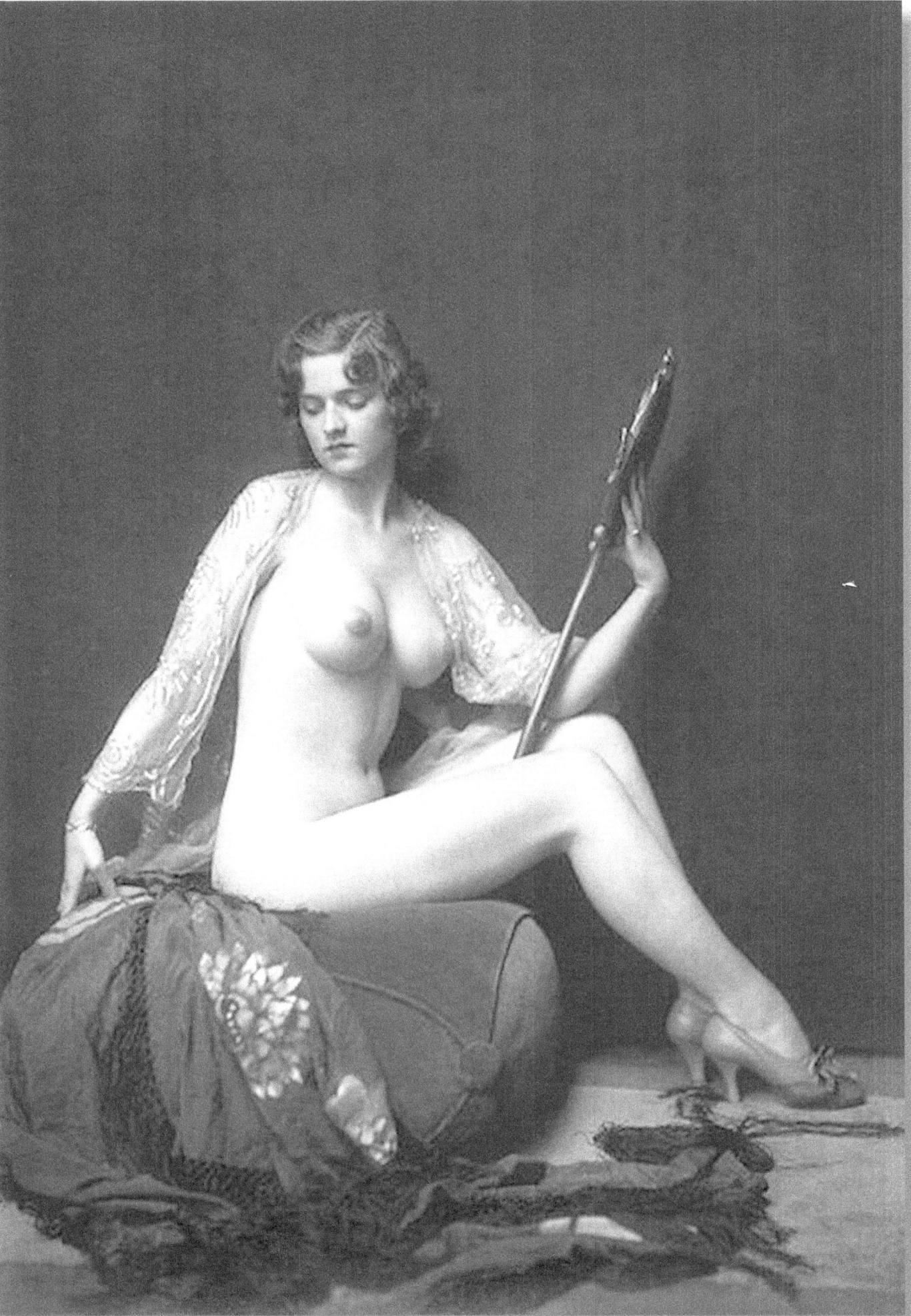

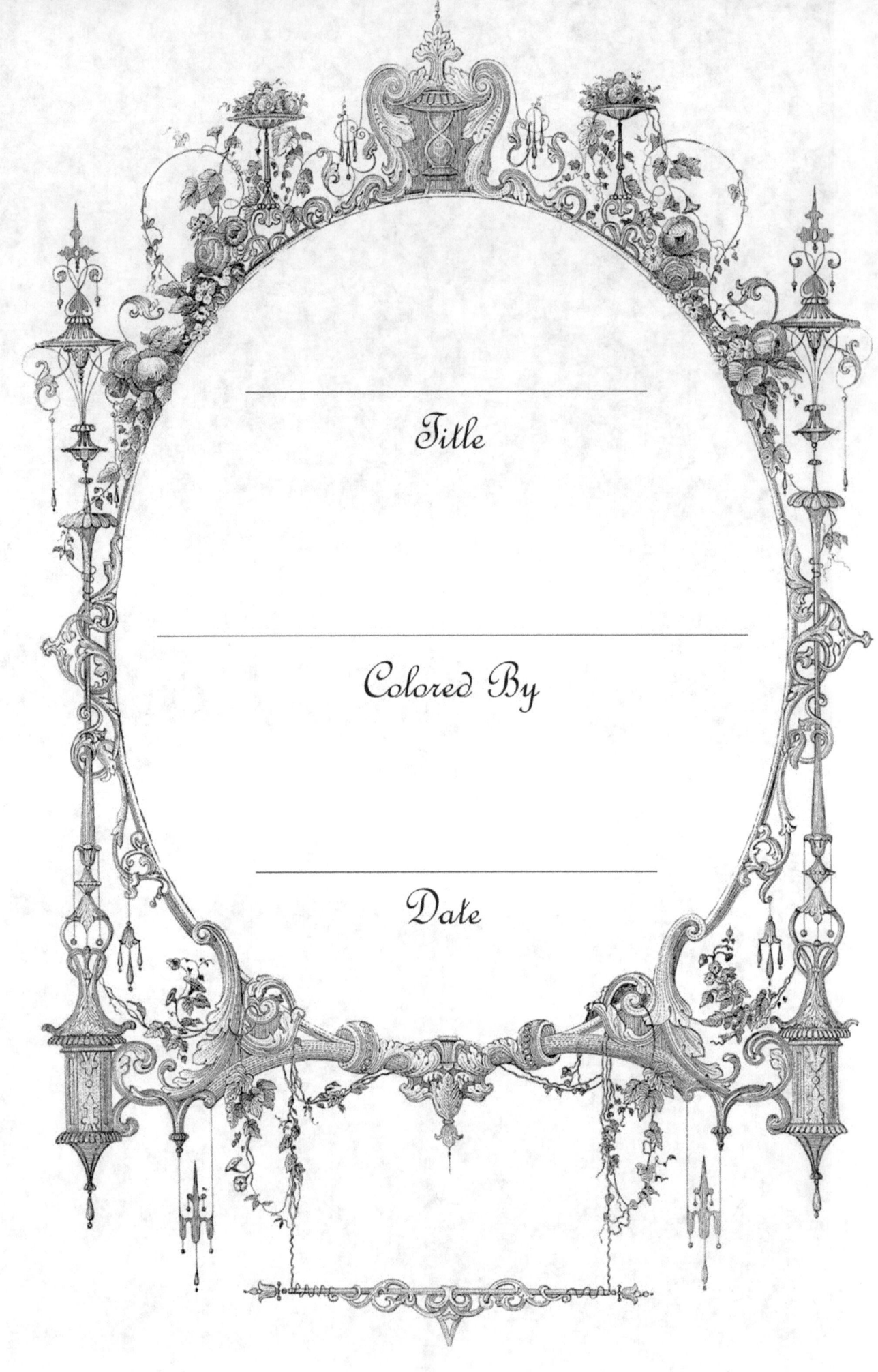

Title

Colored By

Date

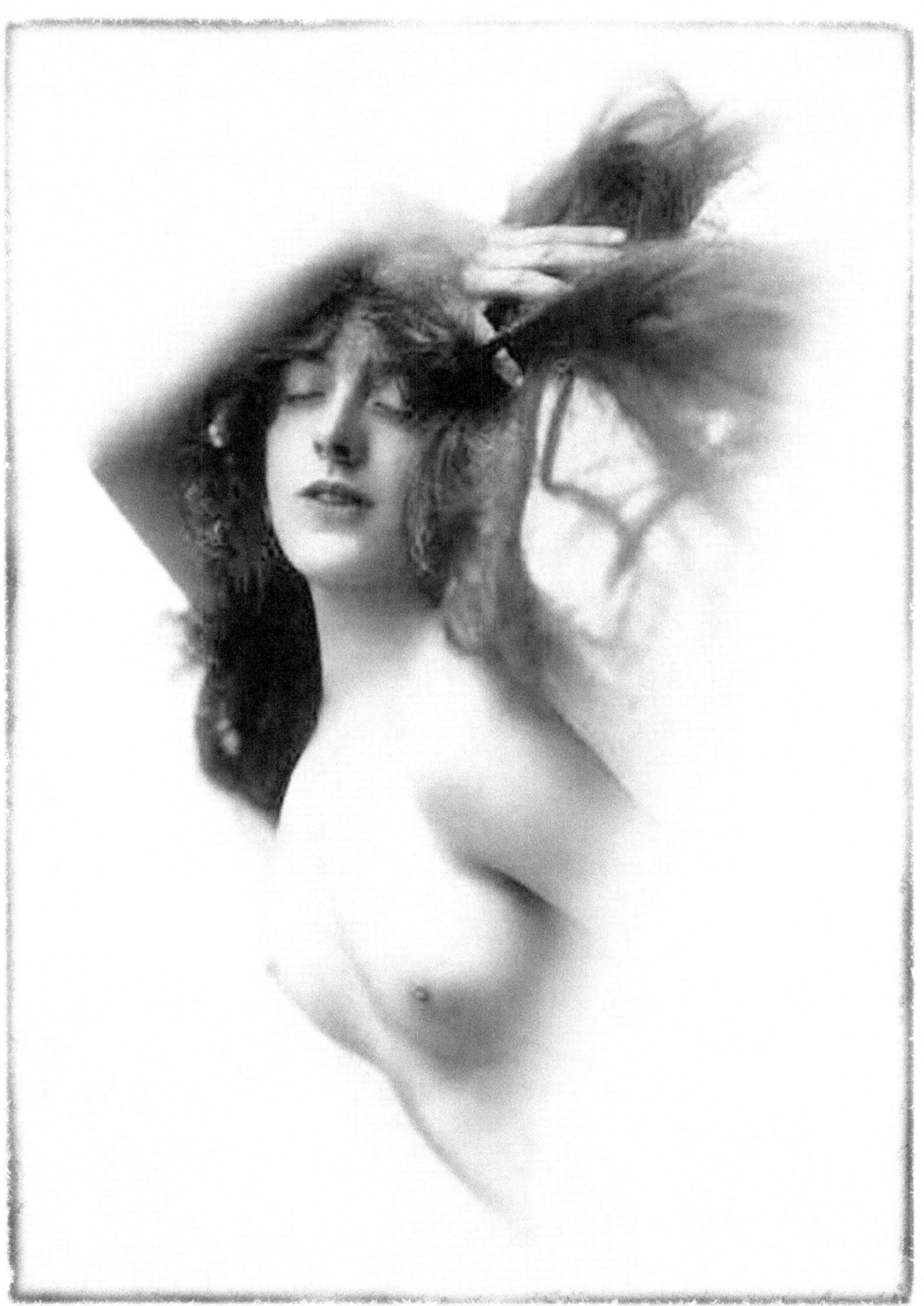

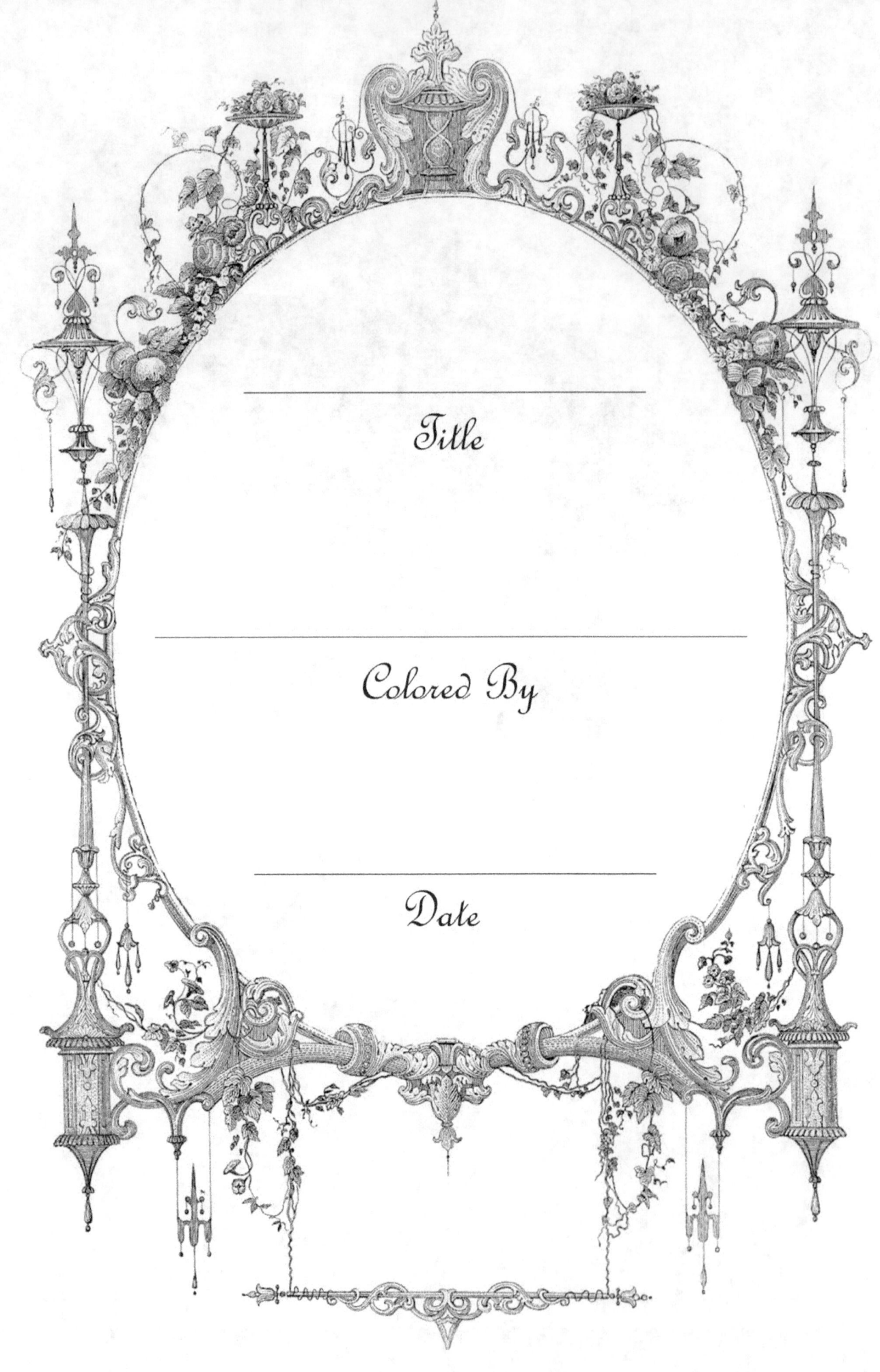

Title

Colored By

Date

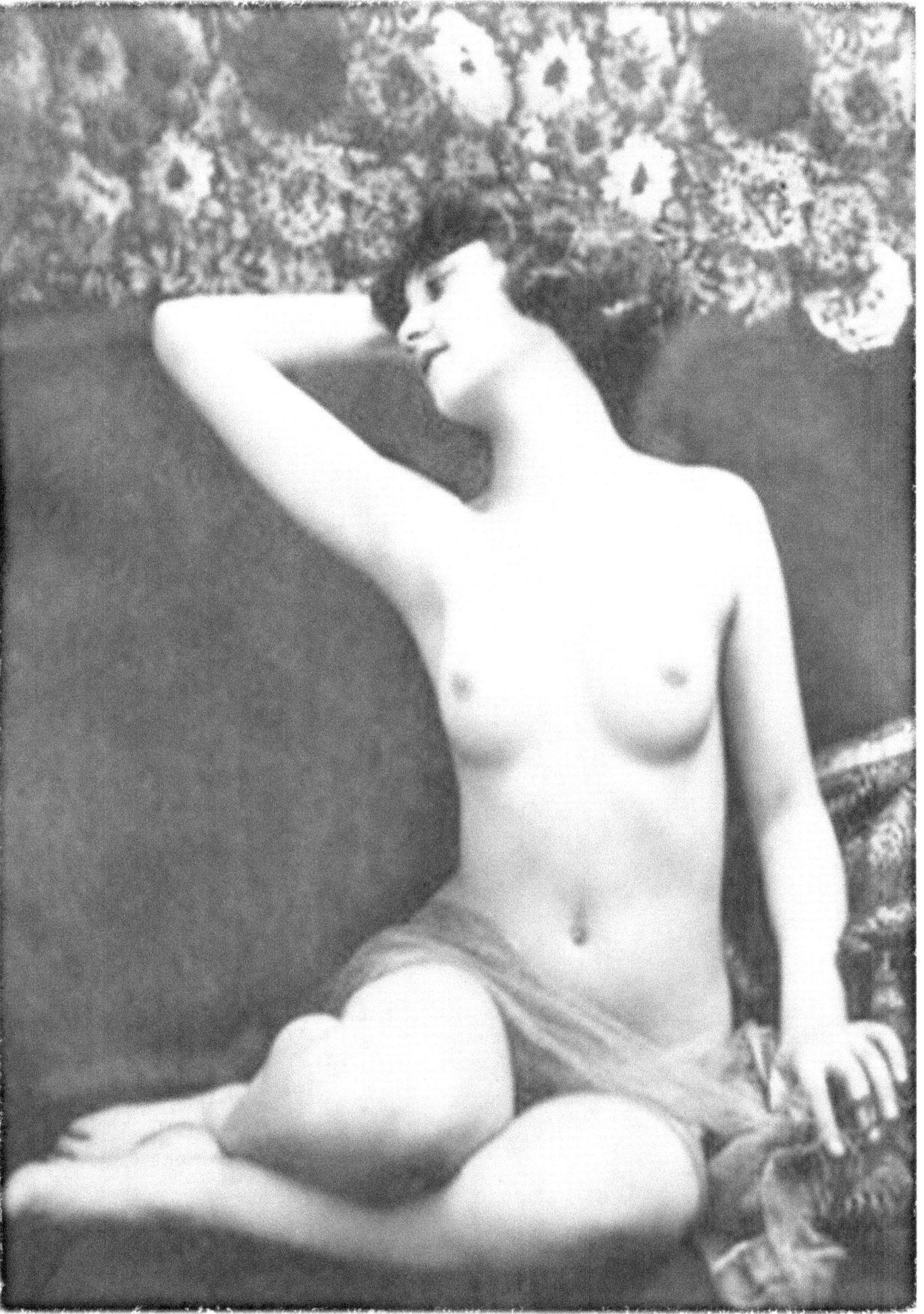

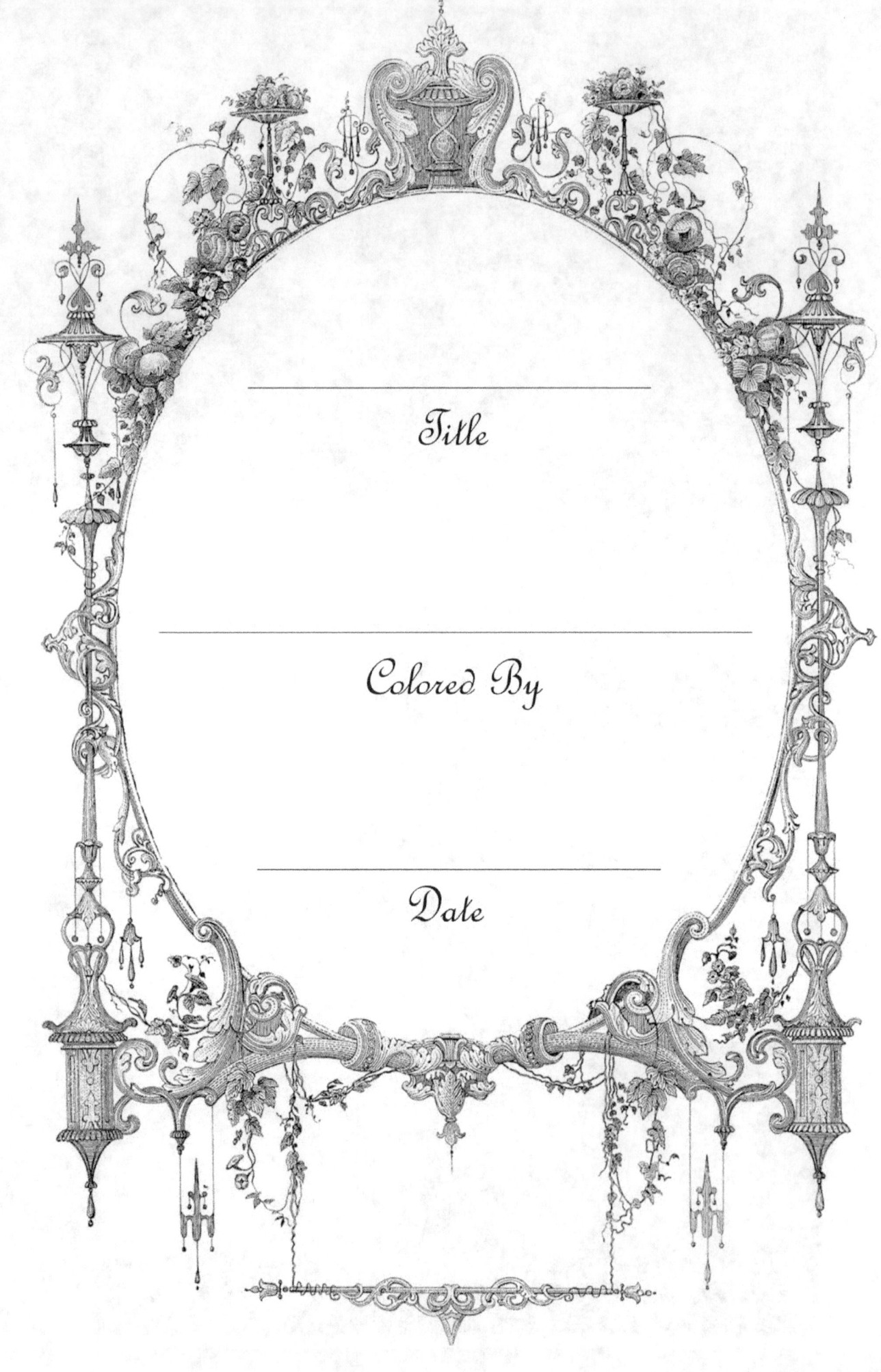

Title

Colored By

Date

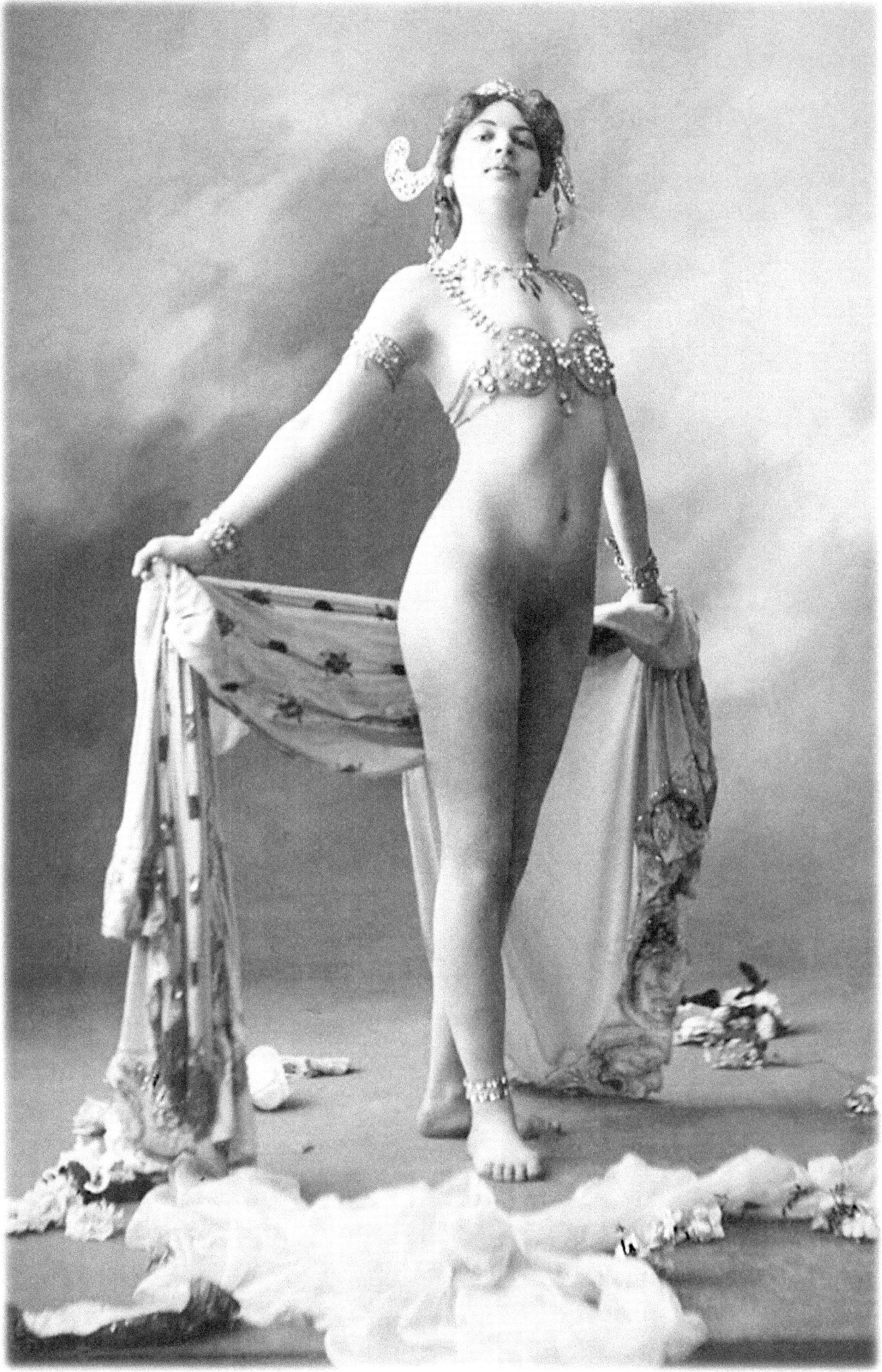

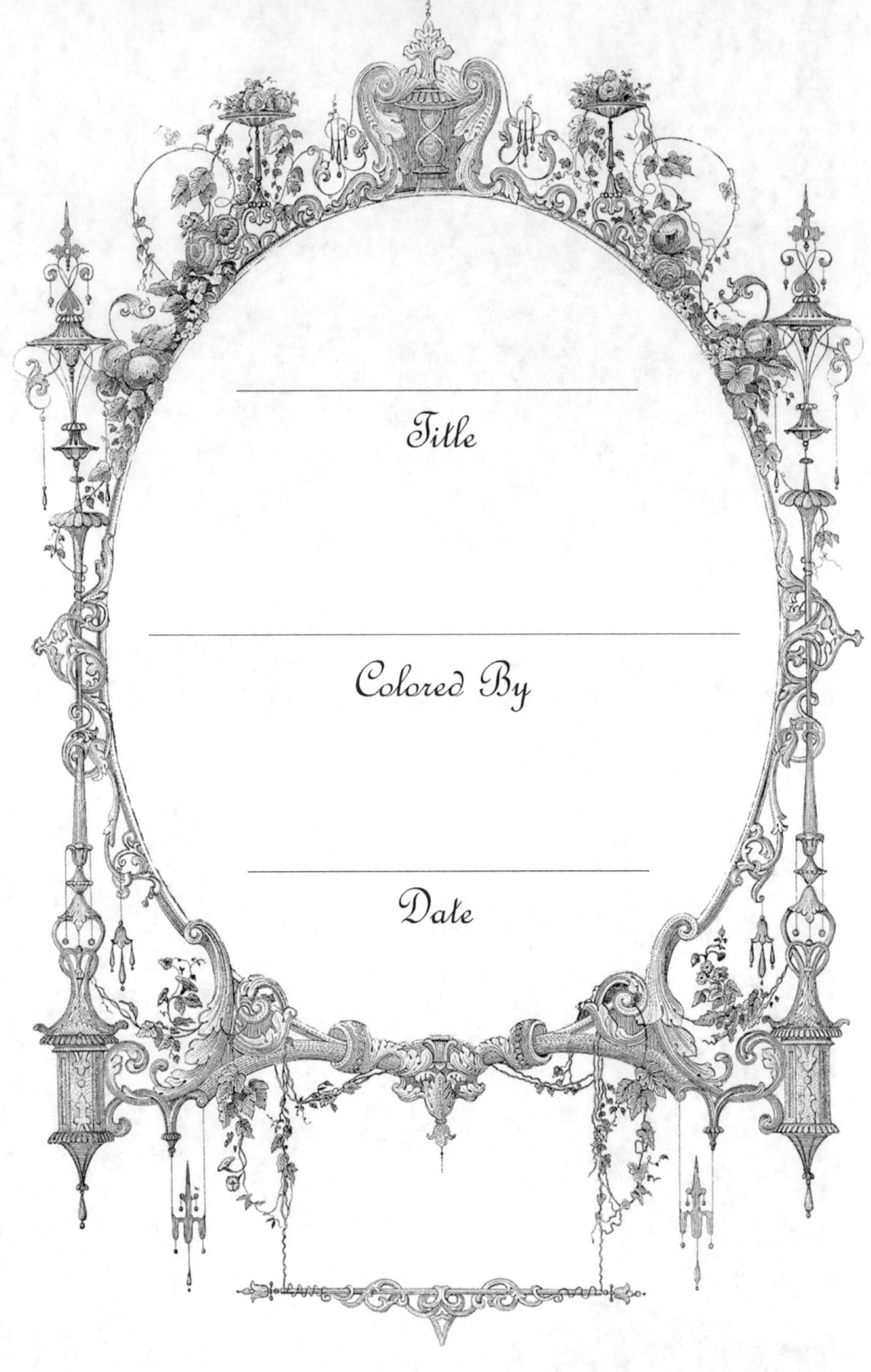

Title

Colored By

Date

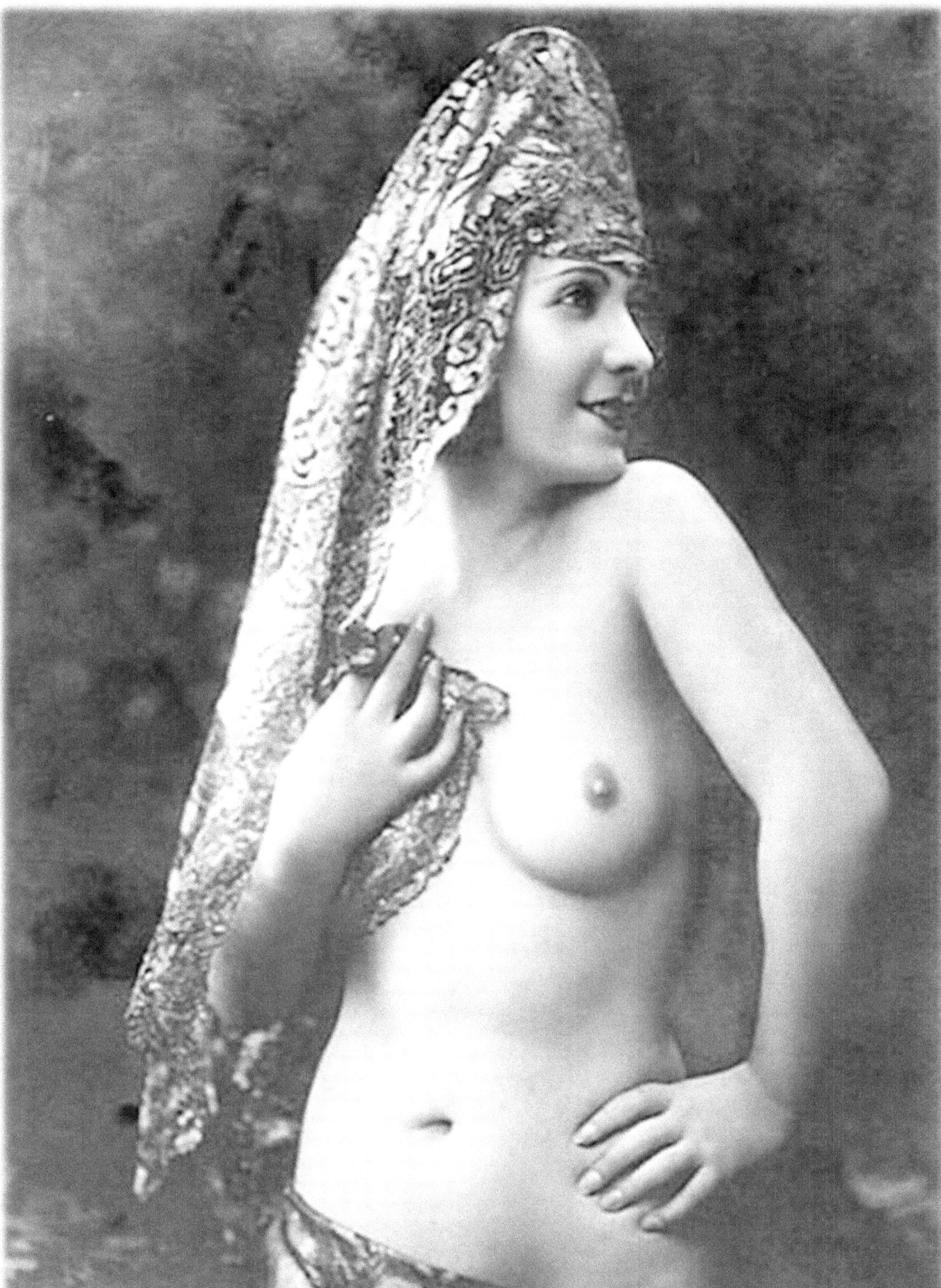

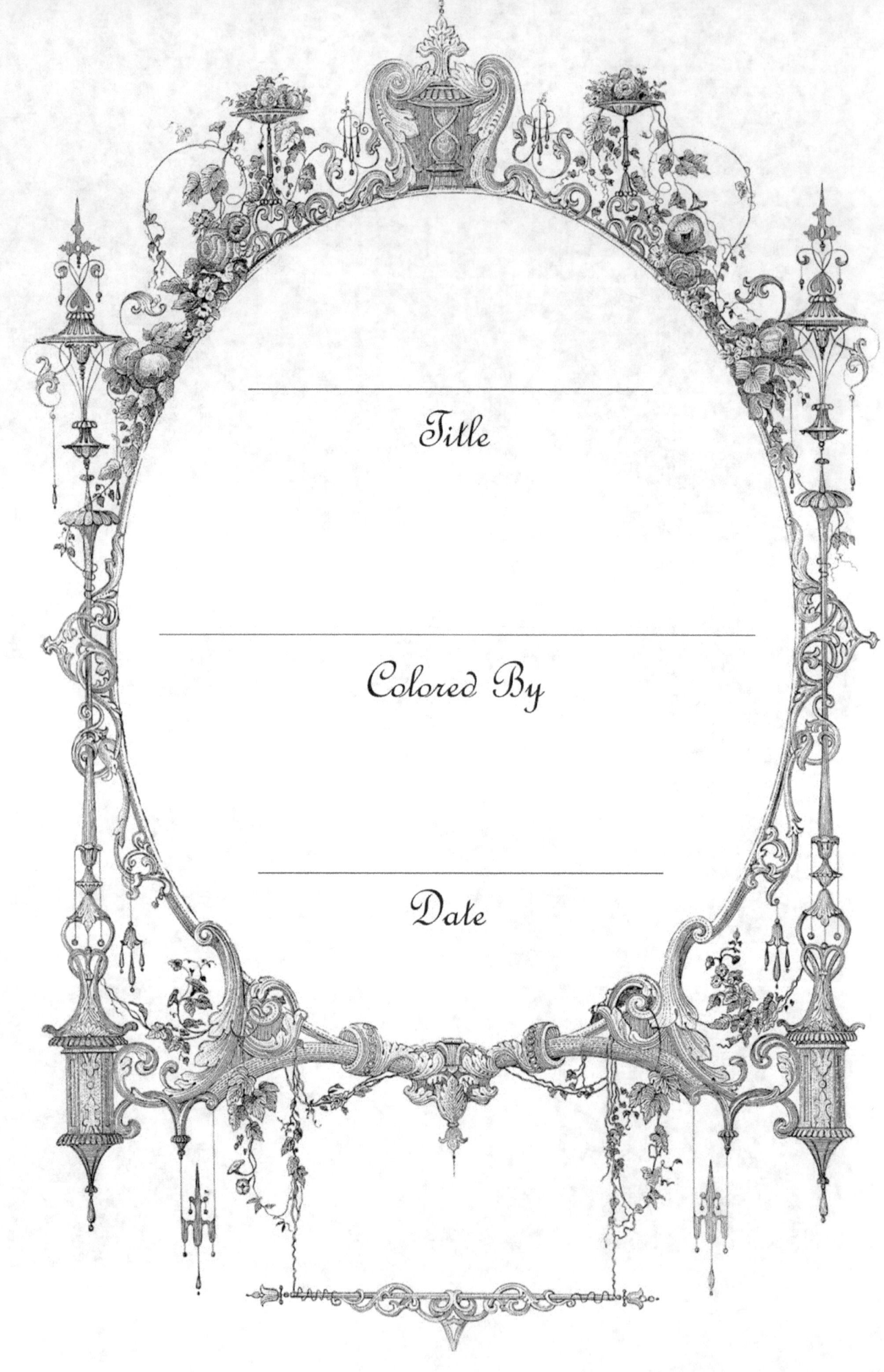

Title

Colored By

Date

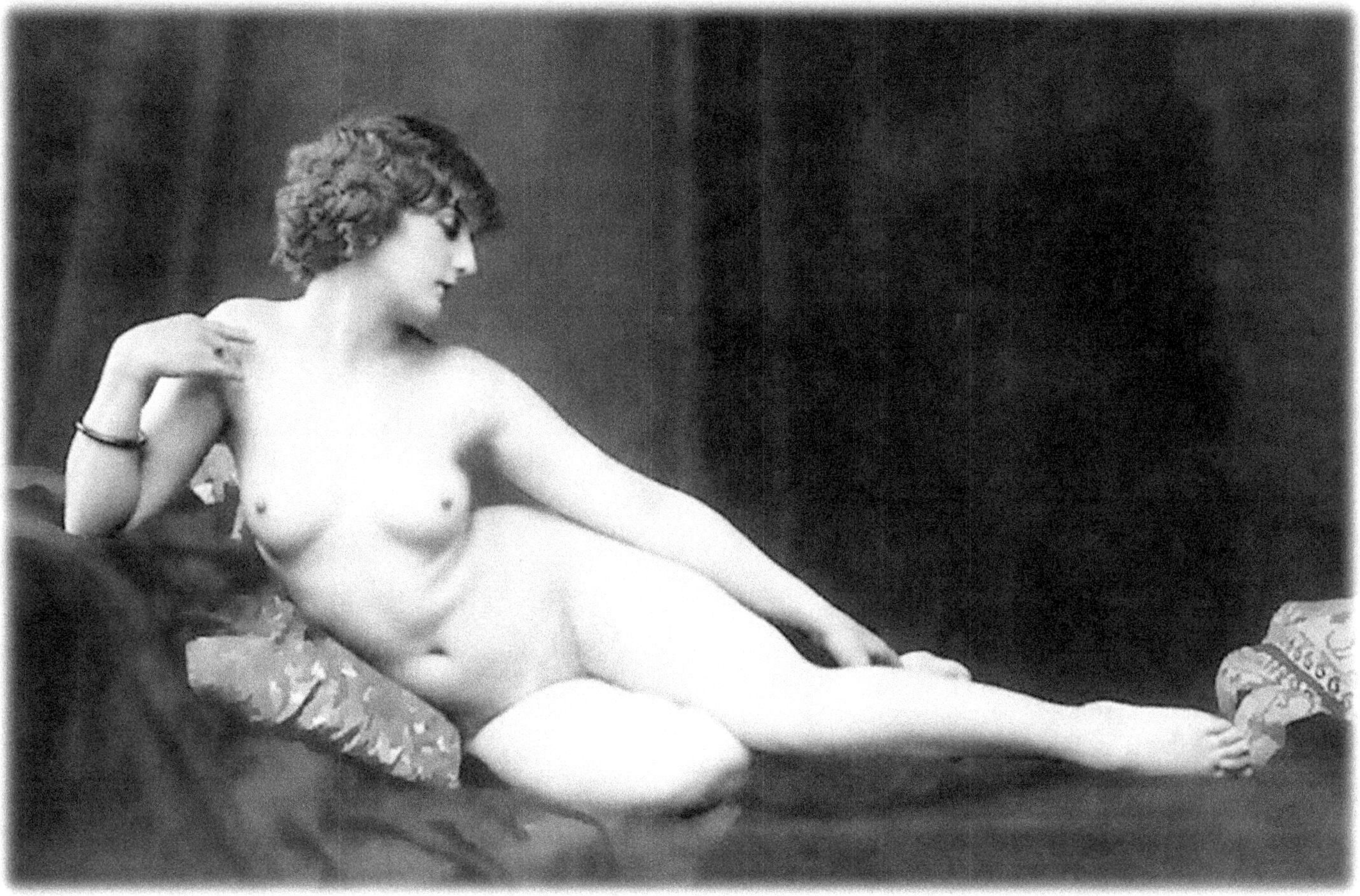

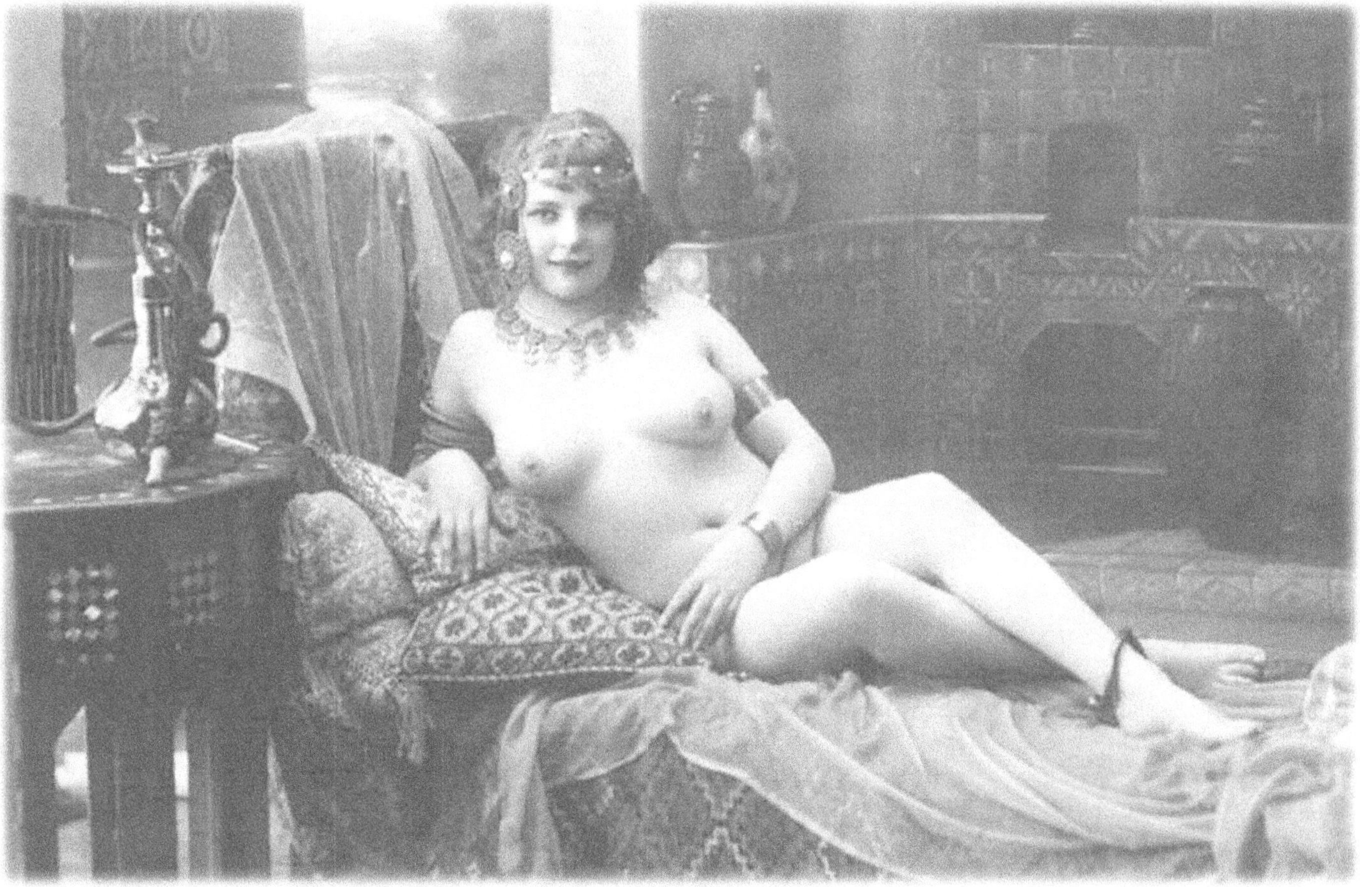

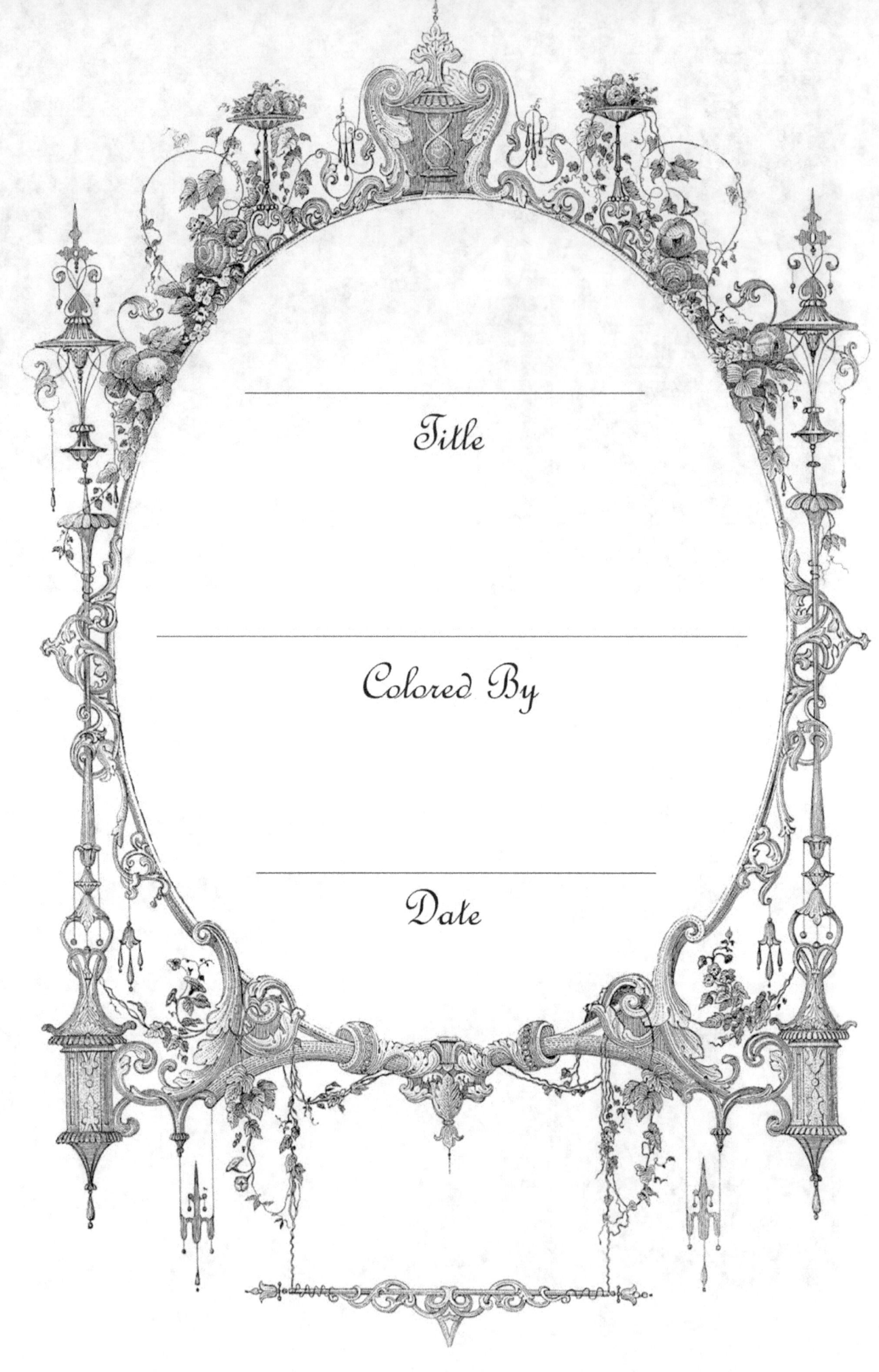

Title

Colored By

Date

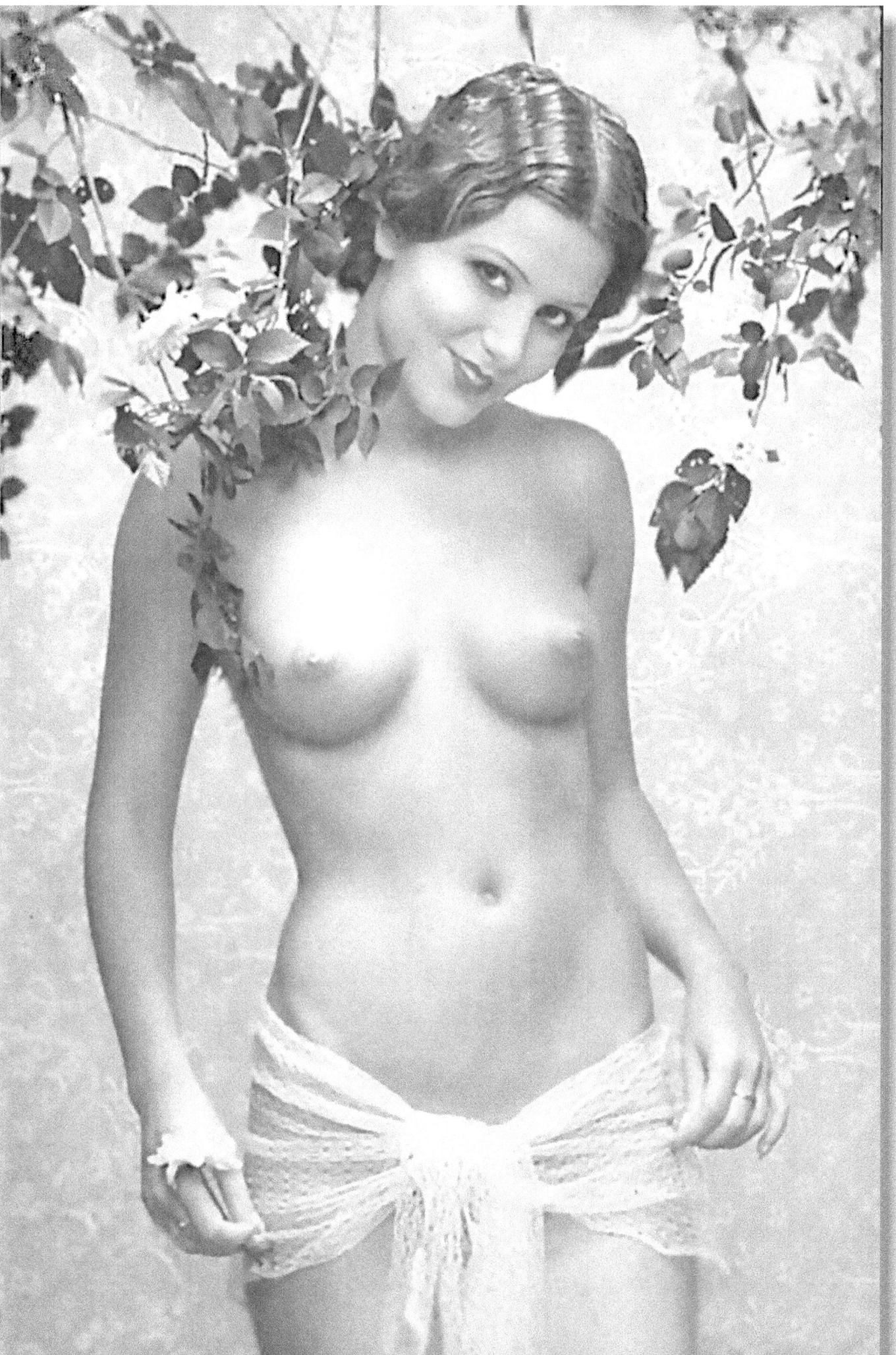

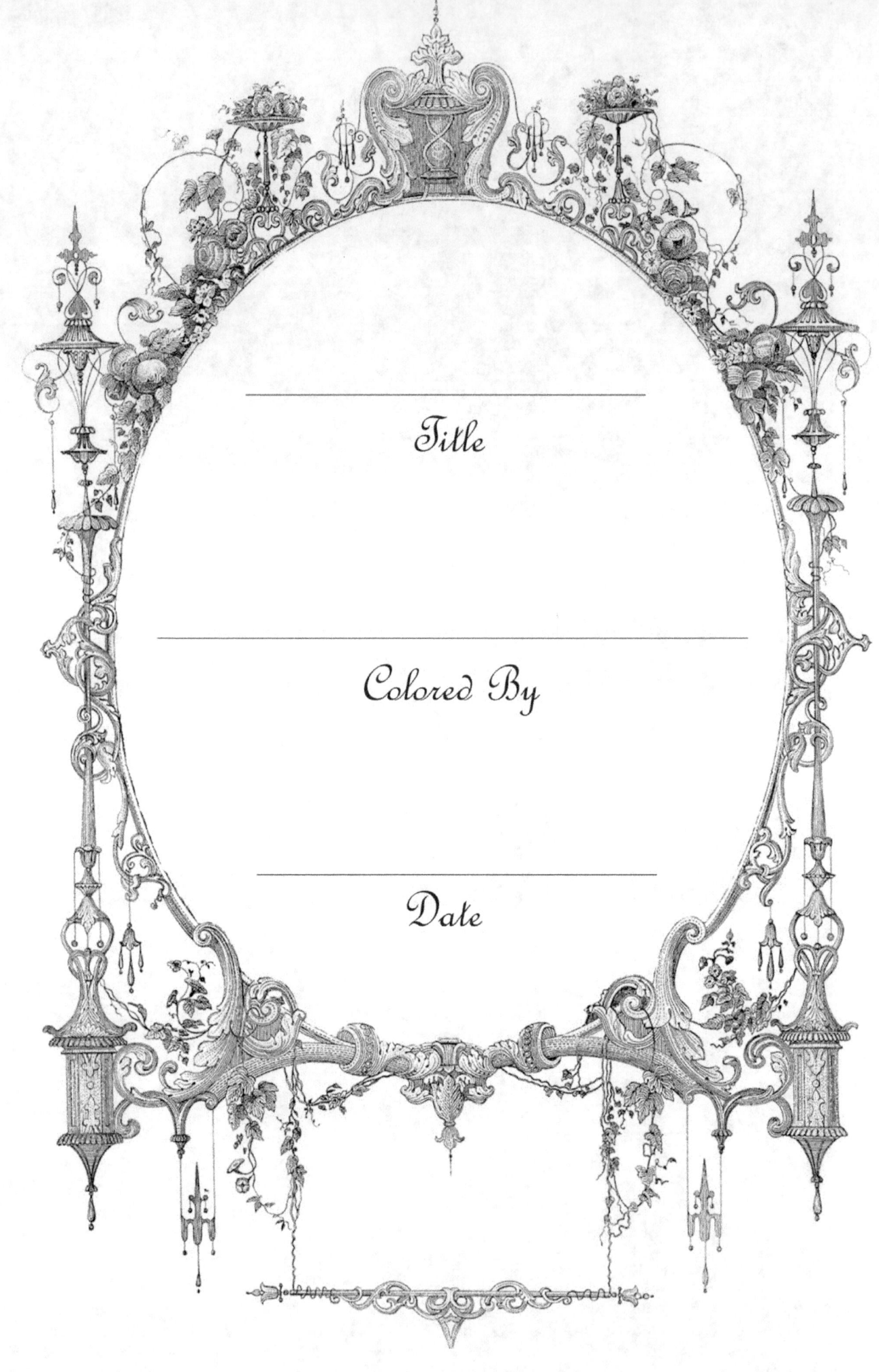

Title

Colored By

Date

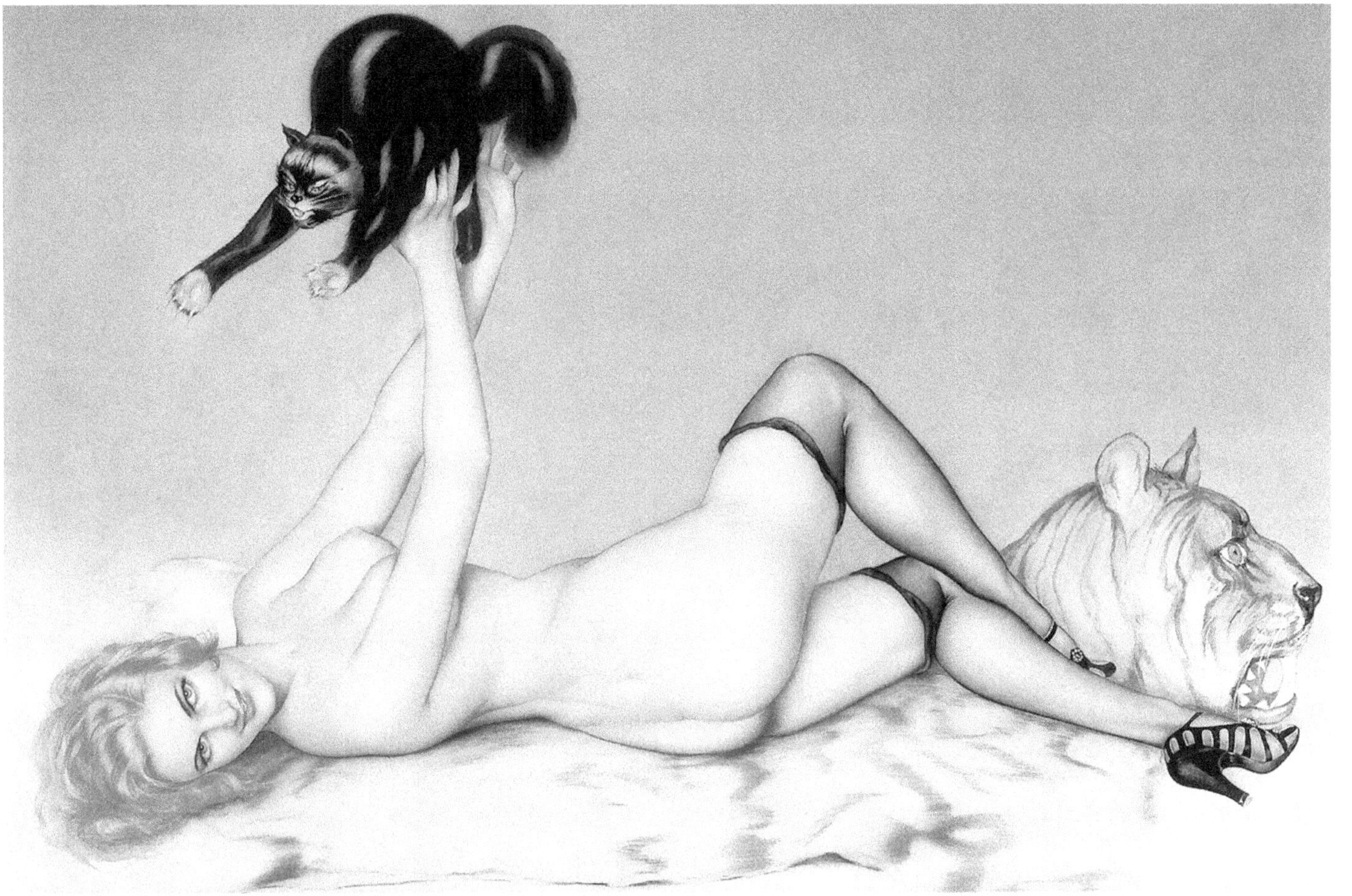

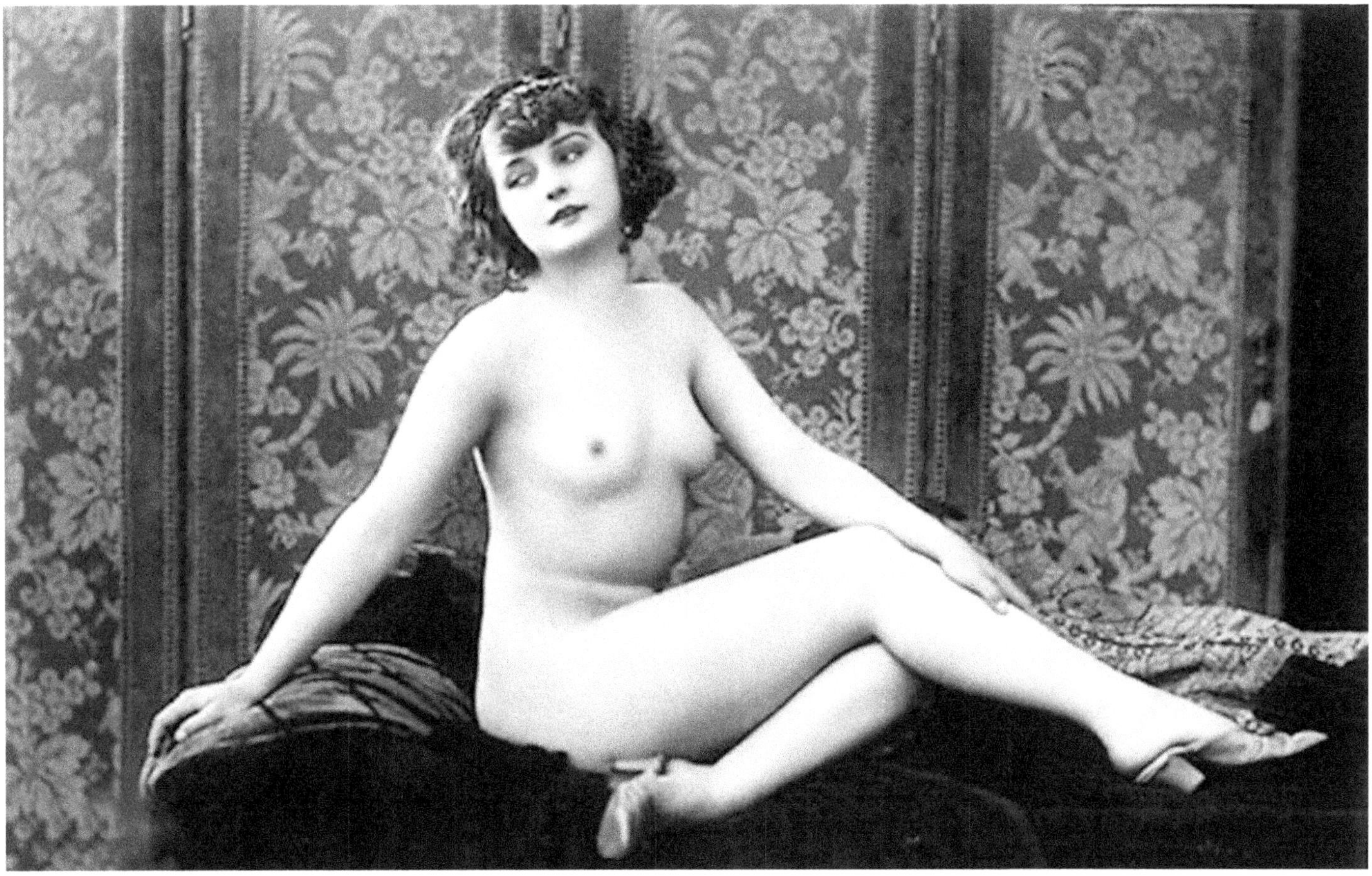

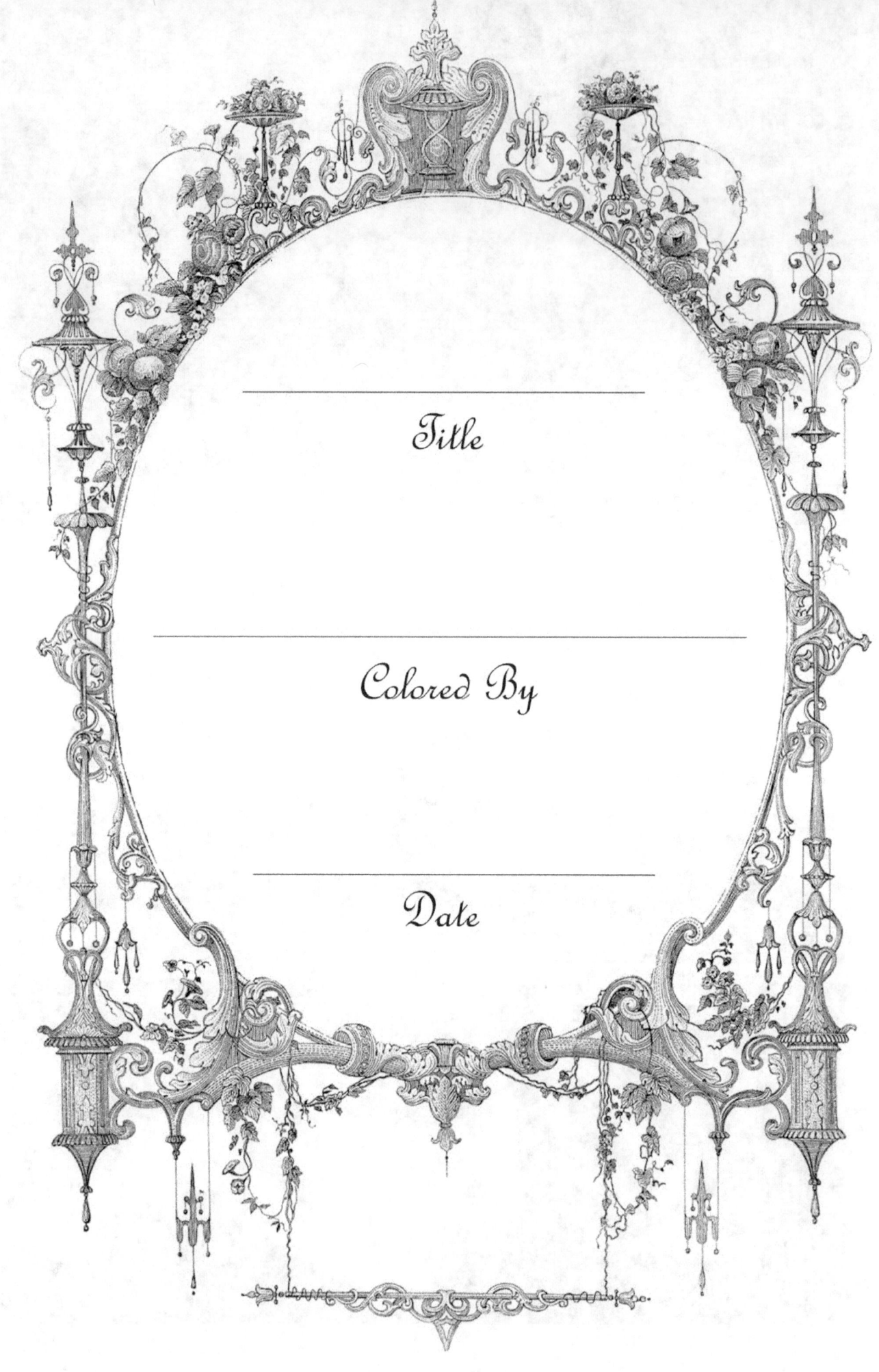

Title

Colored By

Date

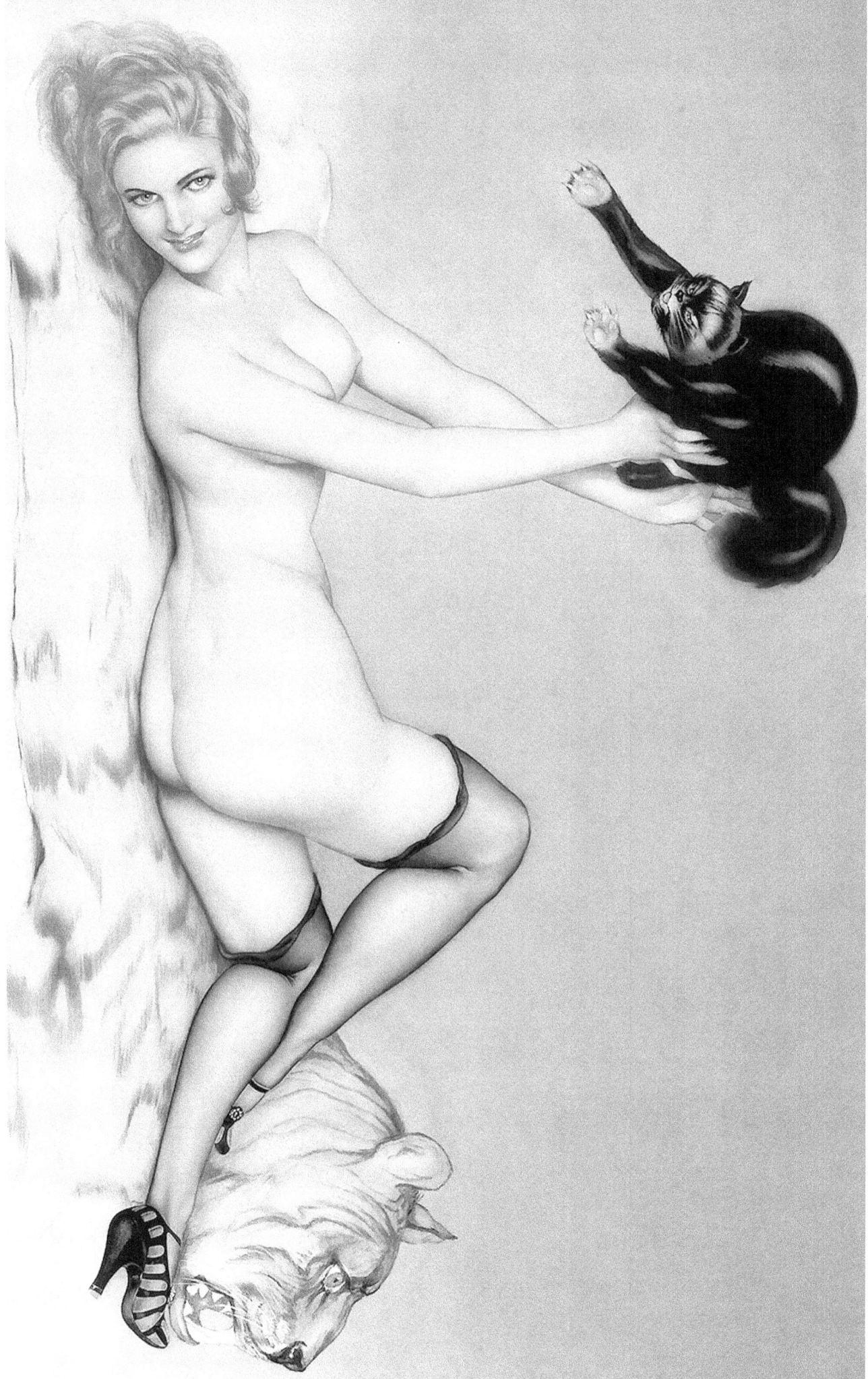

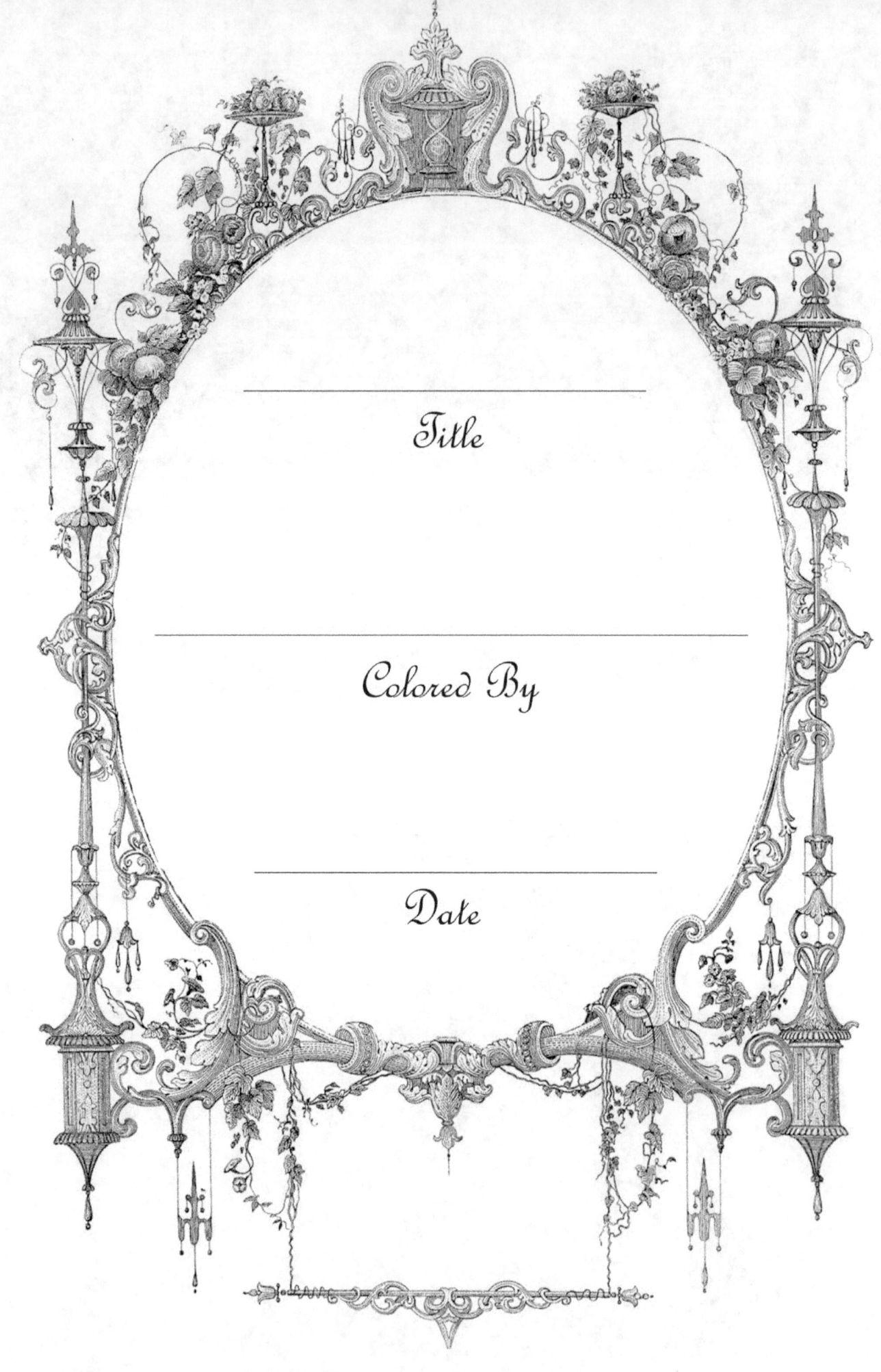

Title

Colored By

Date

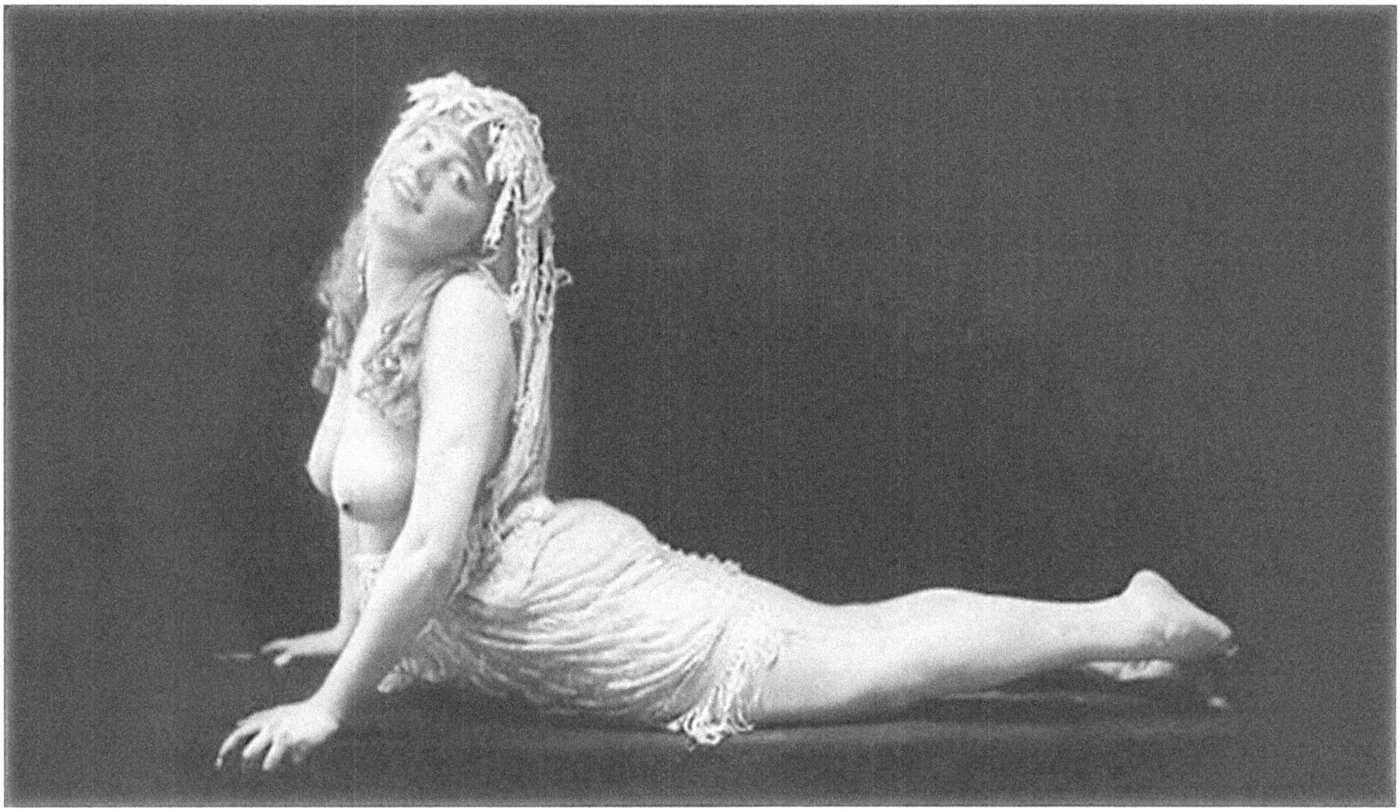

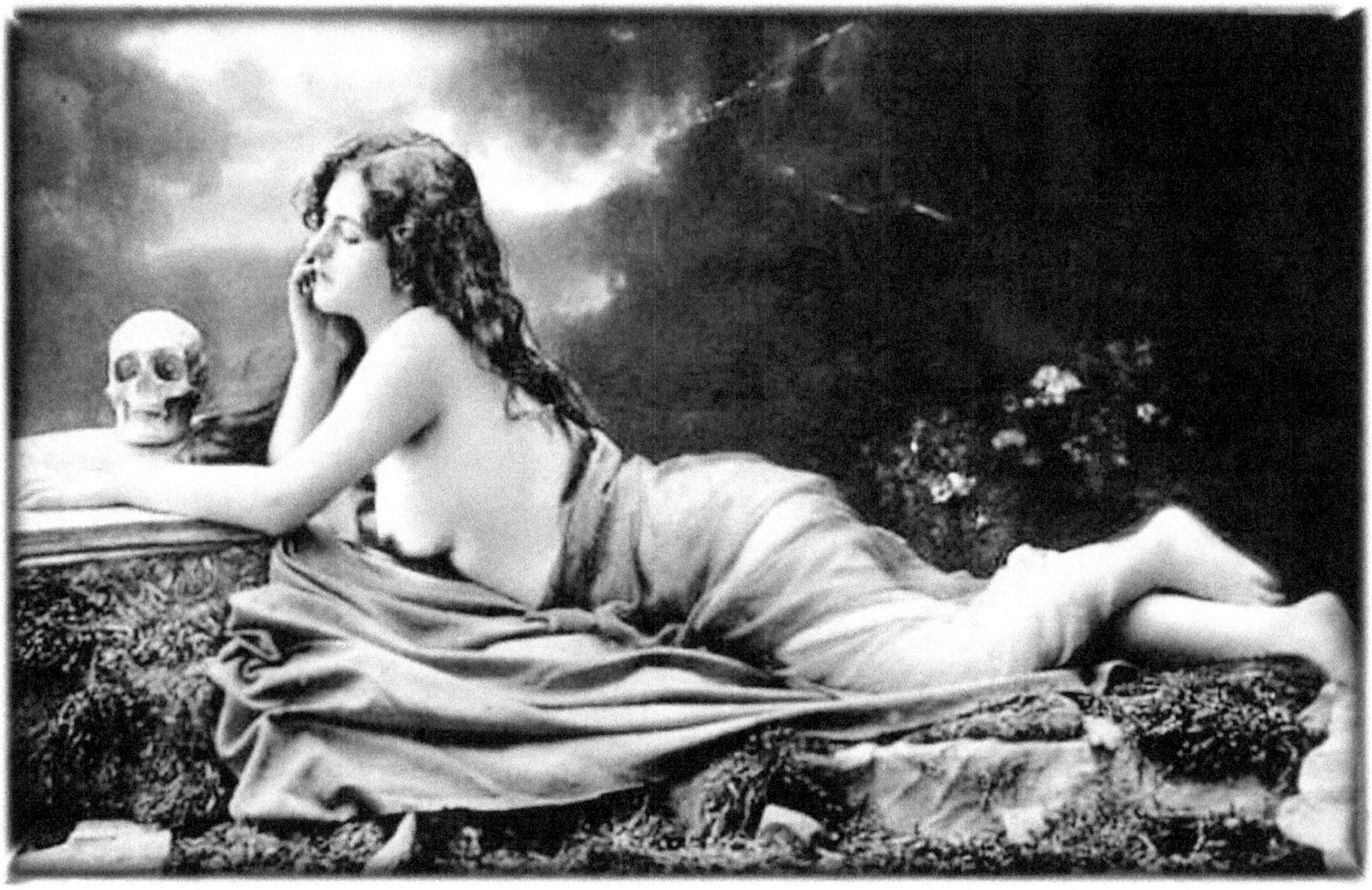

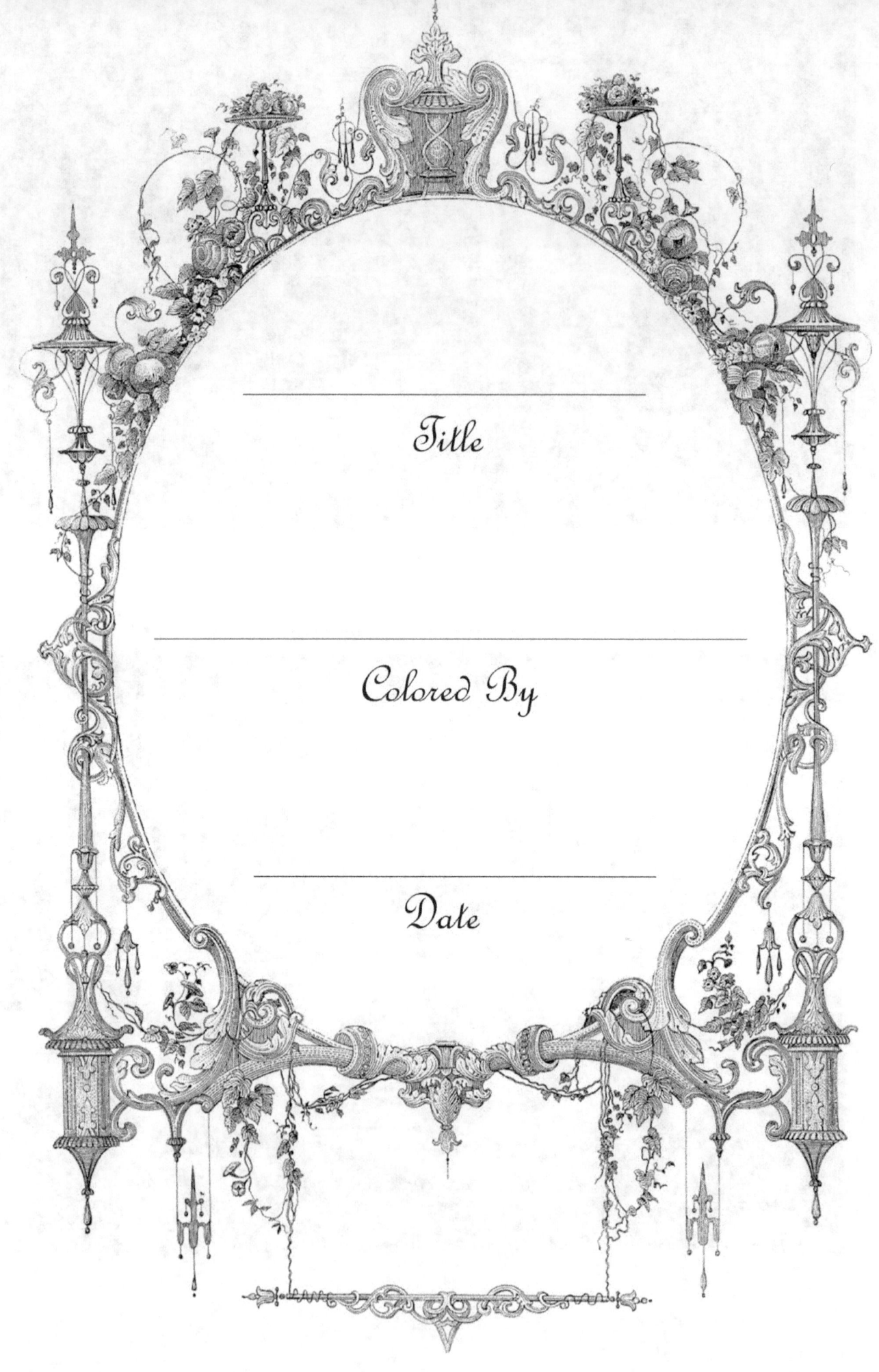

Title

Colored By

Date

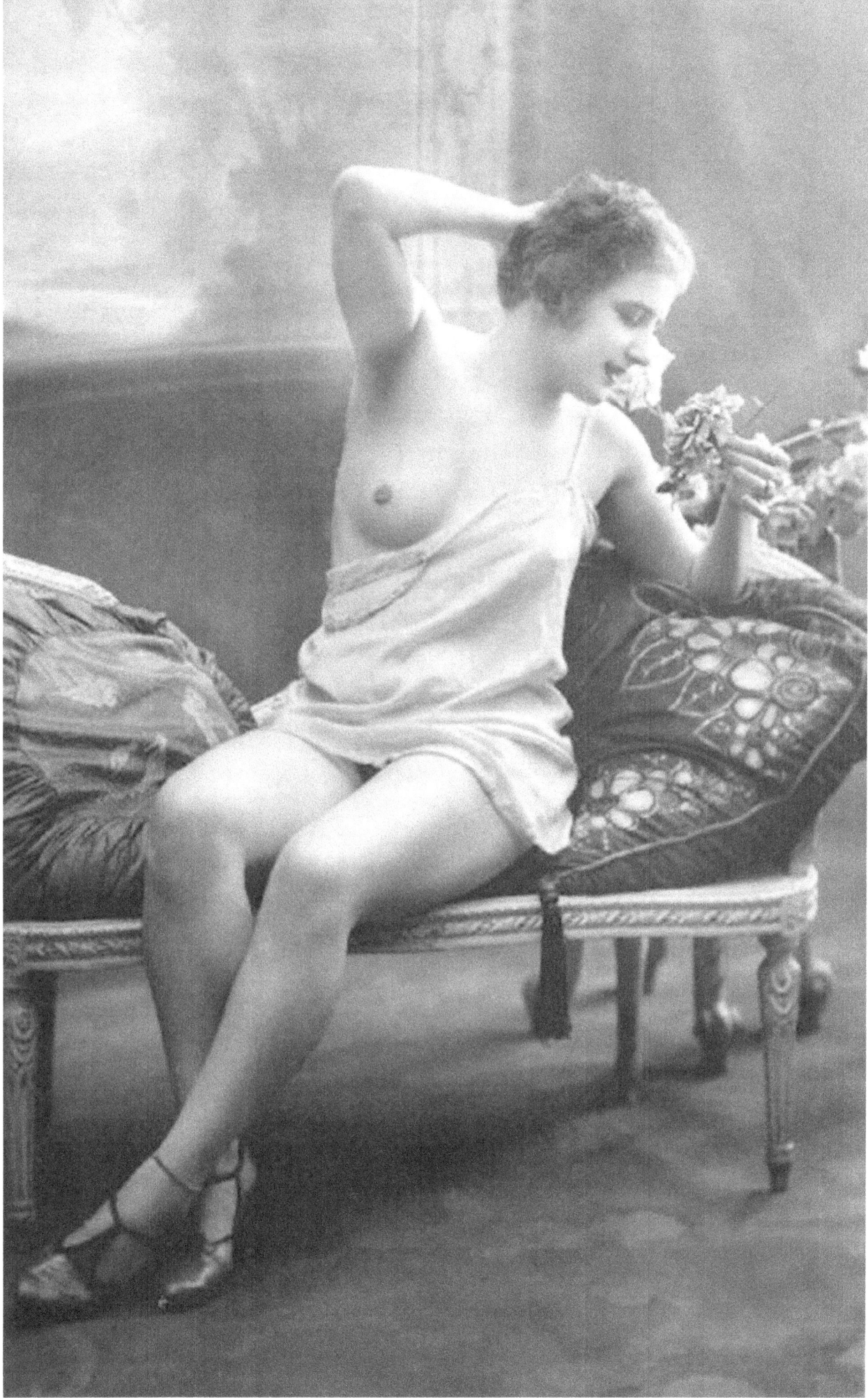

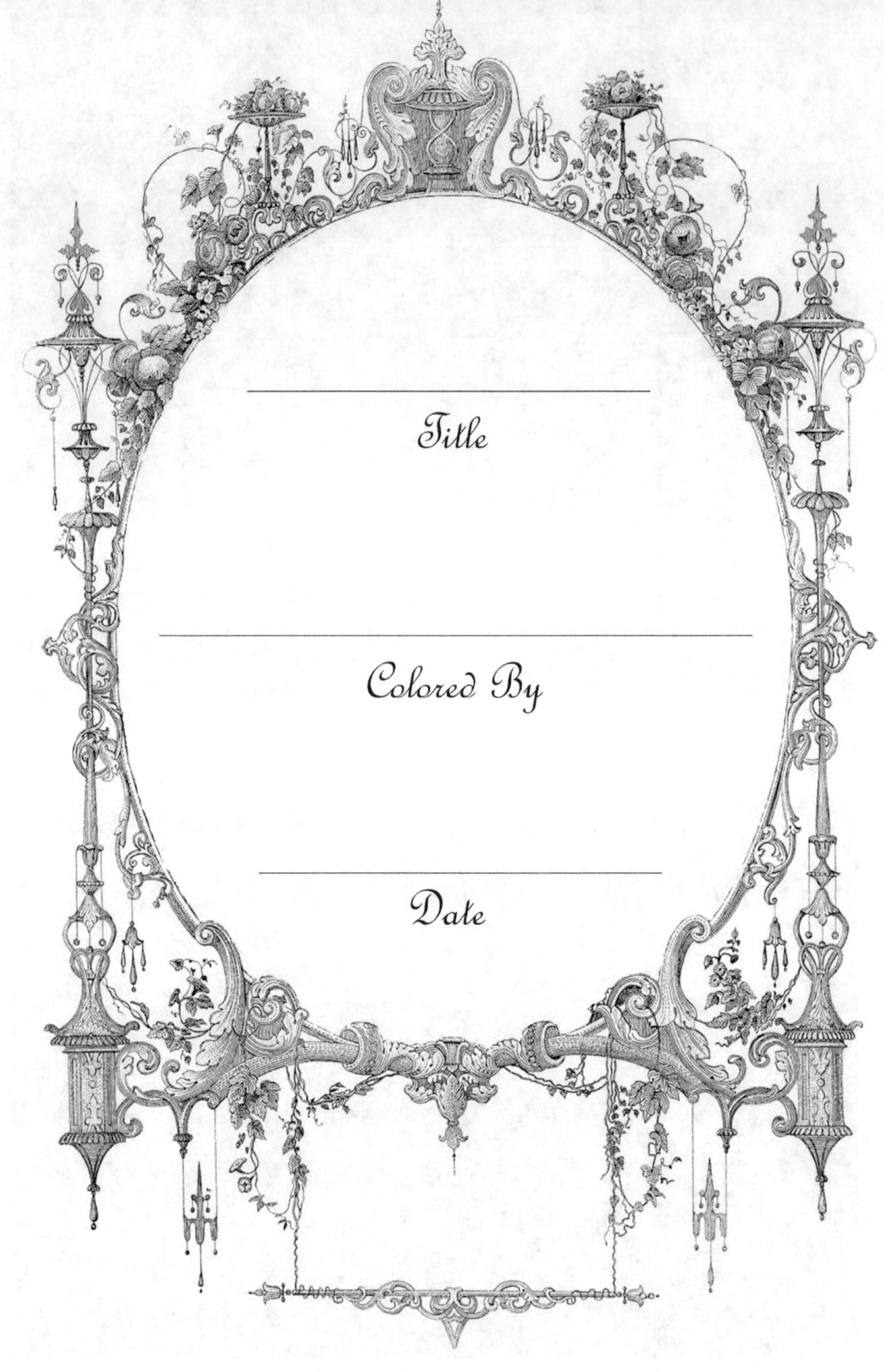

Title

Colored By

Date

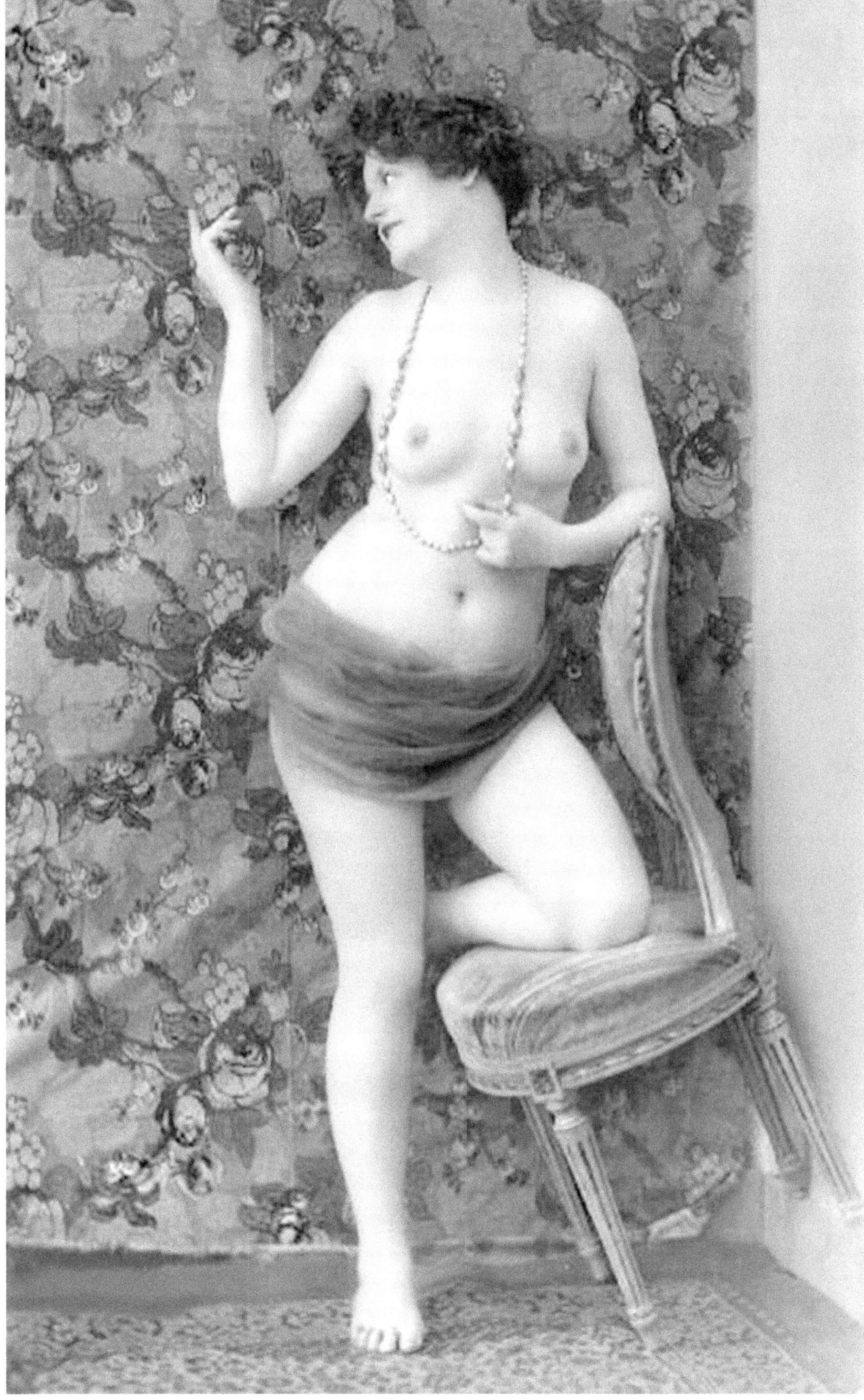

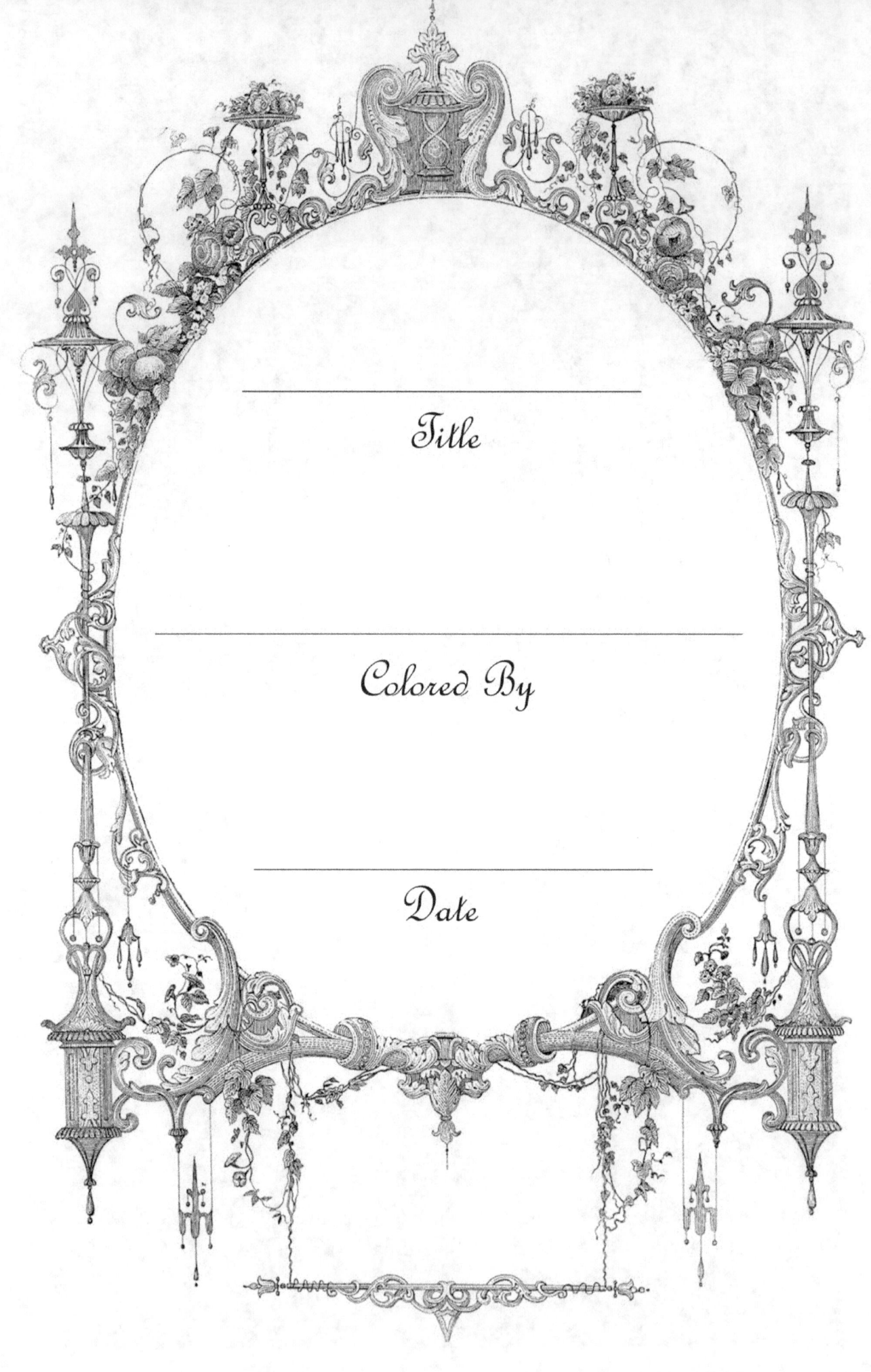

Title

Colored By

Date

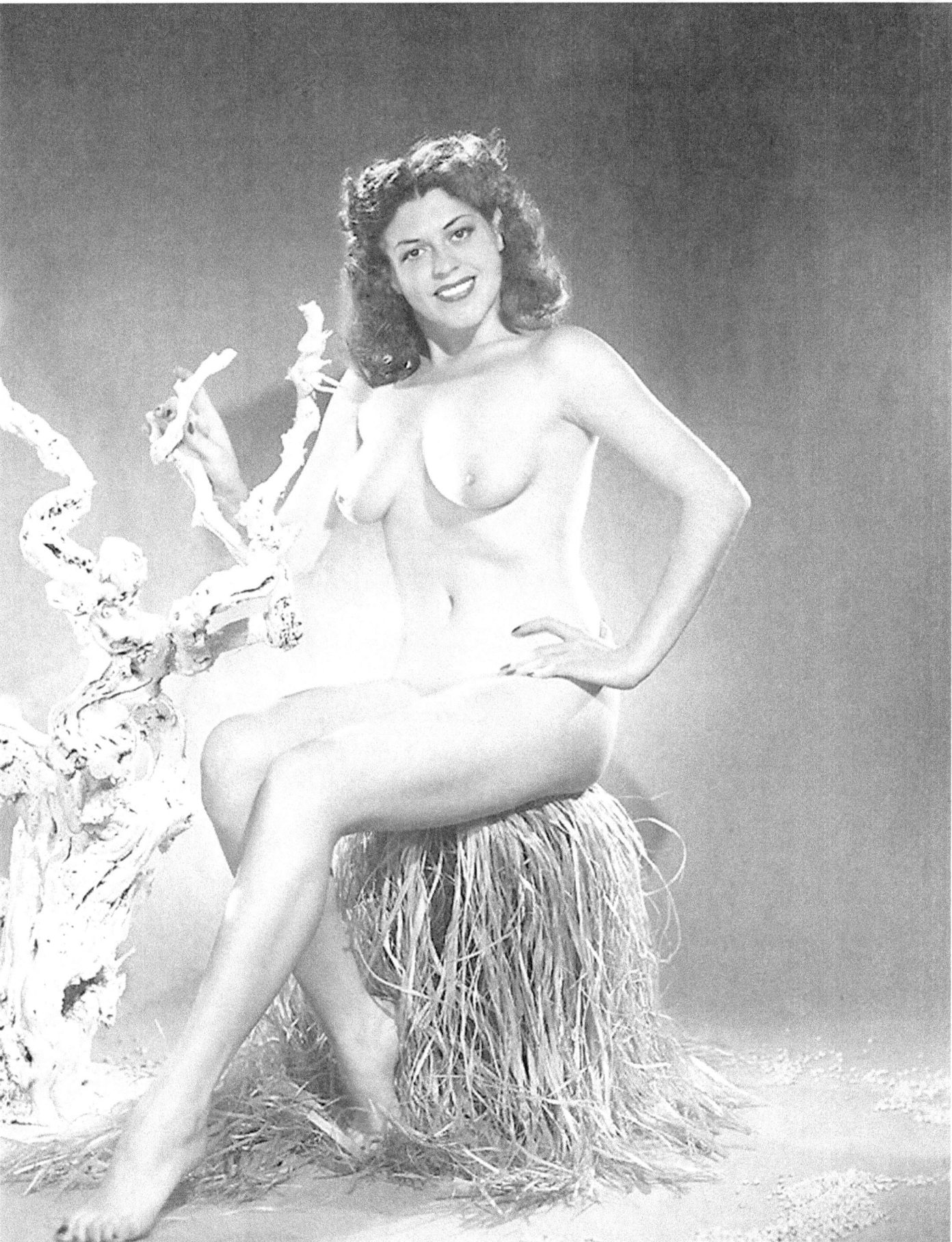

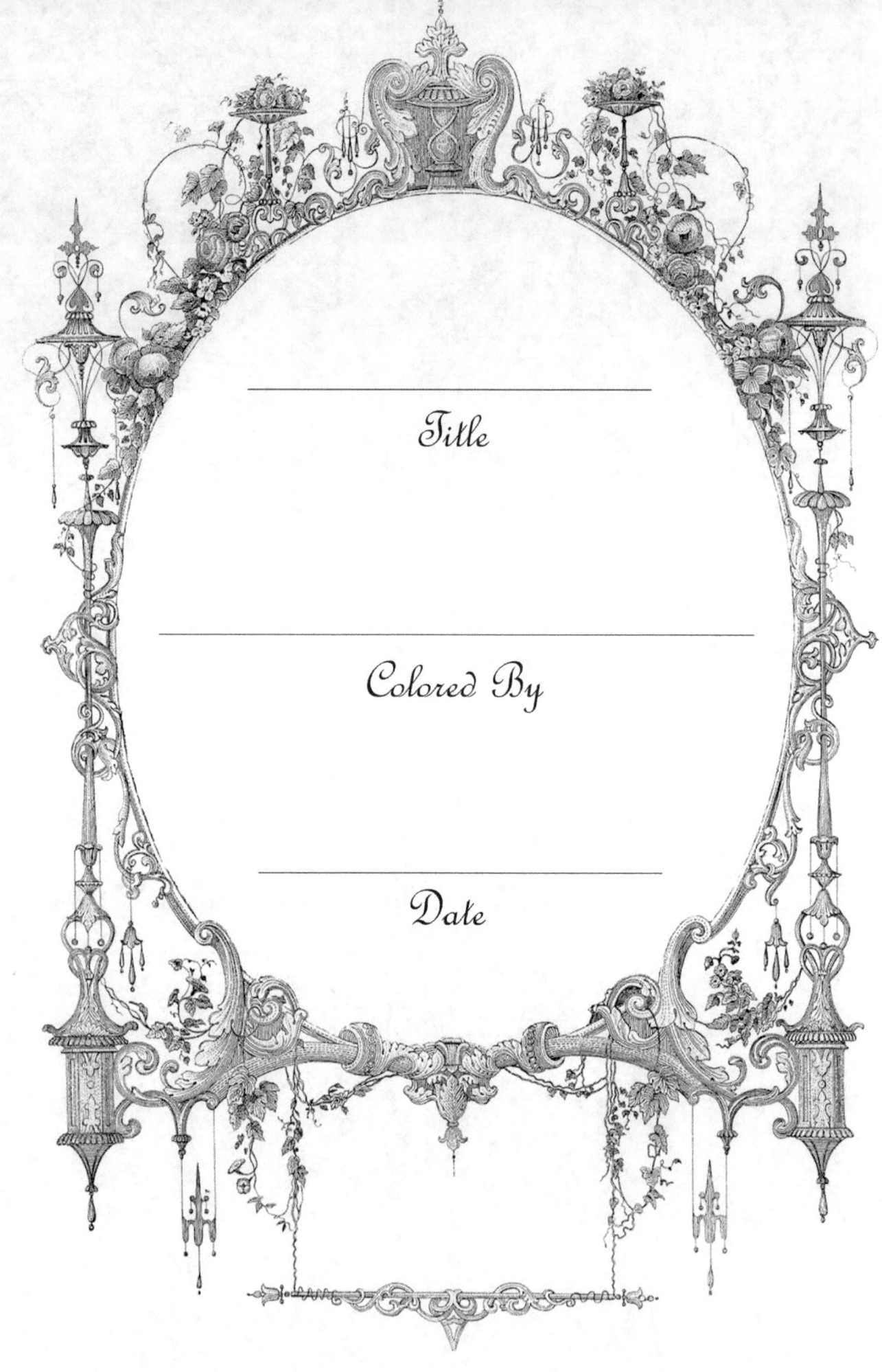

Title

Colored By

Date

www.ingramcontent.com/pod-product-compliance
Lightning Source LLC
Chambersburg PA
CBHW080522190526

45169CB00008B/3025